T H E
CALLING

Praise for The Calling

" *The Calling* is truly a gift from the Divine...to brighten our path and ease our journey home. This book sings with a clarity that illuminates our true purpose here on earth. The wisdom within the pages spoke to my heart...and my heart rejoices "

Jannah Loigman
Greenville, South Carolina

"You have put words to what my spirit has known for eternity. I feel I have come into a Light, a Ray that has found its Source. Thank you from the bottom of my heart. "

Dolly Stephens
Lawrenceville, Georgia

"The words of *The Calling* are impeccable. They are powerful words of purity, of Universal Light, and the truth vibrates on the heart strings of my soul and awakens my remembering. "

Linda Graff
Lancaster, Ohio

T H E
CALLING

Amitabh

As received and transcribed by
Rasha

Earthstar
PRESS

1-800-243-4562

First Edition
Printed in the United States of America

ISBN# 0-9659003-0-4

To every blessed
teacher and guide who,
in walking beside me,
helped me come
one step closer
to home.

CONTENTS

PART II

PART III

PART 1V

INTRODUCTION

Many have called out in prayer for answers and insights into the experience of transformation that has become a fact of life in these times. Many have undergone radical changes that have shaken their very world to its core. And it would appear that many still flounder, unaware of the underlying cause of the upheaval in which their lives have become enmeshed. It was very much a part of the Divine plan that teachings be provided from the world of Spirit that reach into the essence of those issues and touch the very heart of the transformational process. These teachings have been provided, as an outstretched hand, to those in the throes of that transition. For, as you will come to understand, you are, most assuredly, not alone.

Much has been written that would put into historical perspective some of the underlying dynamics that formed the foundation for what is transpiring in the microcosm and macrocosm of your world. These monumental changes, now occurring at an unprecedented rate of acceleration, have left many unprepared for the life-altering events taking place simultaneously within the depths of the planet and within the depths of those who are attuned to her accelerating vibration. We have chosen to return to your realm in consciousness to address those concerns, and provide practical guidance that might not be available in any other way.

In the years that have transpired since the original transcription of these teachings, there has been considerable speculation, on the part of some who feel they have a vested interest in the identity of this source, to dismiss the possibility that we would choose to return in these times in this way. In so doing, these ones have provided for themselves a forum for examining their own fears and frustrations with the limitations of a structure within which they struggle to find relevance. Caught in the dramas of radical spiritual transformation, one experiences a pressing need to integrate theoretical understandings with the down-to-earth practical applications that life and living provide. Those concerns were not addressed in the practical detail now needed, a generation ago, when a large body of metaphysical understanding was provided by this source, in this way.

As with so many attempts throughout history to impart information relevant to times at hand, the teachings that were provided came to be embodied as yet another religion that deifies the messenger and dogmatizes the sacred essence imparted. It is absolutely essential that the distinction be made at this juncture between the Divine teachings that were provided and the structure imposed by a hierarchy that grew in grandeur in the name of that message.

We have chosen to return in consciousness in these times to translate the essence of that information into practical terms that can be applied across barriers of culture. We have chosen to provide the straightforward guidance that is so needed in these times, outside the structural hierarchy of any organized religion. For these times represent the transcending of such concepts and the cohesiveness of uniting in Oneness with all of Creation. We would not limit our own participation in these times to any one cultural or spiritual perspective, but will continue to speak through sources such as this one, in order to provide the breadth of understanding these times require.

From the inception of this communication, we identified 'ourself' to the channel as a "collective group consciousness." And for the duration of our work together, we helped her in her struggle to transcend her need for the comfort of a "name" with which she could pinpoint the scope of this source. As her own personal process culminated in the publication of this work, and as the fullness of her understanding came to fruition ...and she came to embody this training, having lived it ...that name was, at last, provided. We are Amitabh. And we are here with you now.

We come as teacher and as friend, to help you navigate the rapids on which you ride, toward a destination that, perhaps, you have only begun to fathom. This lifetime is the culmination of everything you, as a soul, have done, everywhere you have been, every thought, every nuance ...every blessed breath of your eternal being. The present identity, within which an unprecedented metamorphosis transpires, is the one which will ultimately carry you to the heights of human experience ...if you choose to go. These teachings are provided ...as a love offering ...to those who have chosen to embrace that challenge.

We are Amitabh, God of Infinite Light. And we are here with you now.

PREFACE

The volume you hold in your hands is the culmination of my own voyage of discovery. It's a journey that began in relative 'innocence,' in the summer of '87, when a 'voice' whispered, " I love you," one glorious sun-drenched afternoon.

As I basked in a breathtaking lakefront panorama, my mind became consumed with the absolute 'perfection' of that moment ...the sheer beauty of the nature surrounding me. I remember becoming aware, as I was drawn ever deeper into an almost indescribable feeling of joy, that my breathing had slowed down. It was as though I were detached from and observing myself, as each breath came ever slower, ever deeper, and an extraordinary feeling of pleasure grew, involuntarily, within me.

The 'voice' definitely got my attention. It wasn't audible, but was there in thought. And it surely wasn't _my_ thought! In those days, I had just begun to be aware of such things. By then, I had been practicing a highly devotional form of energy work, of Japanese origin, for several years, and had seen enough otherworldly phenomena there to know there was more to reality than the here-and-now. I had even attended a group channeling of Archangel Michael, a few weeks before, which had left me relatively awestruck. But, as for the idea of "hearing voices" myself ...that was pretty much out of the question. So I thought.

"I love you," the voice repeated. This time, I KNEW I had not imagined it. Something else ...SOMEONE else was 'speaking to me' in my mind. "Are you my Higher Self?" my mind replied, tentatively, not quite believing what was, indeed, happening. "No," the voice replied, "we are not you." Thus began a 'conversation,' in silence, during which I was given detailed specifics of an ancient, past-life connection with an incarnate expression of 'the voice,' who identified "themself" as "Rama," the Hindu God. I was told that I had been a channel in countless previous lifetimes. And that I had volunteered to serve the Light as a channel in THIS lifetime ...that it was, in fact, my life's work.

I was flabbergasted! This was surely NOT anything I had ever wanted to do. Being the consummate coward, while simultaneously priding myself in embodying the responses of a Light Warrior, I collided head on with my own reality. What they had in mind, the voice explained, was for me to transcribe a book ... in fact, several books ...of spiritual teachings. I was dubious. But I agreed to think about it.

So began a seemingly endless summer of evenings which started with "get a pencil," and ended with page after page of fascinating information on everything imaginable. During the exercise, my skills as a channel were being practiced and strengthened. I was taught the importance of calling in protection. And, at "their" suggestion, I graduated from a legal pad to doing 'transcription' on the typewriter.

The process was as natural as breathing for me. Yet, as the information started taking on a decidedly 'heavy' metaphysical slant, all the "what ifs" hit me at once. "What if it's only my subconscious mind?" "What if I've LOST my mind, altogether?" I reasoned that if I could get objective, clinical 'validation' of what was actually going on, I would feel more secure about it.

Thus began a 'search for external validation' that would become the recurring theme over which I would continue to stumble for the next ten years. This round, I sought out the 'official' opinion of the head psychiatrist at the local university medical center, who was intrigued and agreed to see me, absolutely gratis!

I presented volumes of amazing material for his scrutiny. He devoured the writings. And, under the deluded impression that I had a mainstream "Good Housekeeping Seal of Approval" pending, I continued to visit twice a week, at his insistence, and continued to dodge his suggestions that antidepressants would make me "feel better." In the end, they didn't. I never did transcribe Rama's book. Instead, I spent the better part of six months curled up in a ball, getting on and off medication that didn't agree with me. By then, the focus of the exercise was obscured. And thoroughly confused, I decided that channeling was not for me!

A year passed. And over breakfast, a dear friend and well-known channel in her own right, with whom I was staying, presented me with the invitation that would change my life. She explained that an entity had come to her and 'requested permission' to speak through me! My answer was an instant "No thanks! I don't want to be a channel." Undaunted, she replied, "Before you decide, let me tell you who this being is." I listened, as she extended the formal invitation of the very source of the teachings that formed the foundation of the Japanese spiritual organization in which I was, by then, intensely involved. I was stunned. Had it been anyone else, the answer would have been an emphatic no. I decided that I would consider what 'he' had to say. Then I would decide.

That evening, I returned automatically to a process of relaxation, breathing, and calling in protection, that was apparently far from forgotten. And I invited him to interact with my consciousness, if it was his wish to do so. A warmth spread throughout my entire being. A feeling of almost indescribable joy filled my heart chakra. And the irrepressible smile spread across my face, that would become his calling card.

"They" explained very carefully that "they" were a "collective group consciousness" that chose to incarnate in Japan, in a certain time frame, in order to carry out a specific mission. They did not limit the scope of their energies to that incarnate identity alone, nor, was it from the "limited perspective of that identity alone" that "they" spoke with me. Nonetheless, I chose to perceive this presence as the late founder of that Japanese spiritual movement, whose name translates as "Savior" and is regarded as such by over a million devotees worldwide. The concept of that incarnate identity was all I could handle ...back then, in 1989.

From the perspective of that stage in my own process of embracing "the calling," I was not even remotely ready to grasp the magnitude of the consciousness with whom I, in fact, began a relationship that evening. It was a bond with an interdimensional team...of which, I was told, I was an integral part ...that would span the next eight years. I would go on to struggle to grasp the scope of that connection for most of the duration. And the issue of the identity of the one who speaks with you in this volume, <u>became</u> my process. I would go on to live the book I went on to transcribe ...a course in spiritual warrior training that would encompass, trigger, and magnify every imaginable human emotion.

My task was to transcribe a volume of spiritual teachings ...or, more likely, several volumes. Months of testing followed, as the "one who had volunteered, before coming into this lifetime, to be the 'scribe,' amongst the 'ground forces' of an interdimensional mission" (they can't really mean <u>me</u>, can they?) was prepared to 'come on-line.'

For the writings, "they" preferred the practical advantages of direct communication without the necessity of having me channel the material orally and then transcribe tapes and edit them ... a very lengthy and time-consuming process used by many who bring through channeled material. Ultimately, I was to transcribe the teachings directly onto a computer.

Vibrational levels were established that were low enough to enable me to retain use of my hands, so I could type while in trance. Anything higher and, it seemed, I was paralyzed. Yet, of necessity, the levels had to be high enough to ensure the integrity of the communication and to rule out any potential interference from my own consciousness ...or the possibility of the distortion of the material from other sources. It was an exquisite exercise in balance. The fine-tuning was painstaking ...and on-going ...as the importance of insuring the accuracy of these transmissions was impressed indelibly upon me. I worked at it for hours every day, until, finally, it was deemed that I was ready.

The months that followed, in early 1990, were filled with days on end of transcribing teachings that filled me with wonderment. Passages that made me tremble with the profound simplicity of their wisdom. Teachings that put my very own process into perspective, again and again. Truth that brought tears to my eyes. Information that made me think. Issues that made me question. Guidance that made me probe my own consciousness to its very depths ...and then dig beneath <u>that</u> level for the core belief systems which, I came to understand, were holding me back. For every step forward, there always seemed to be a few back. For that is indeed the process.

It was an insular exercise that spanned half a year, as a body of work was documented that would have brought this volume to 500 pages, if all had been included. Awestruck and humbled, I presented the manuscript in its entirety to the Japanese spiritual organization whose very foundations were built upon teachings from the same source. I assumed their blessing would be automatic, in light of who, I believe, authored this work. Apparently, they didn't quite see it that way.

Instead of being embraced for the exquisite content of its teachings, the entire work was dismissed. As a rule, the organization dismisses all channeling as "disturbance," and turned a blind eye to the entire matter. I was devastated.

"External validation," take two. God only knows what I had been thinking, to have approached them in the first place. I wasn't thinking! I was deep in my process ...starring in my own movie. A movie about a book, entitled "The Calling," dictated by an aspect of God him/herself! I was living this book. But it would be years before I would be able to integrate that understanding.

As a means of dealing with the issue, I avoided dealing with the issue. Day by day, for years. During that time, I spoke with Amitabh sporadically, at best. As always, they were supportive, loving, and encouraging. They made it clear that my participation in the entire project was voluntary. And I made excuses. They reassured me that even though a particular direction had been anticipated to "form a thrust of my life script," I was not being forced to follow through. "You are most welcome to choose to continue in the mode of stuckness that you have experienced thus far ...and explore infinite variations on the theme of struggle, if you prefer," they wrote. The truth hit home. After years of dodging "the calling" ...and the book by the same name, neither one had gone away.

I began to reread the manuscript I had transcribed six years earlier ...and shelved. And I found, to my amazement, how all of it still rang true. I found passages that brought my heart to its knees. And left me humbled by the eloquence with which the profound wisdom was expressed. Above all else, I was overwhelmed with gratitude, for the entire process ...agony and all. For I could never have come forth with this work, had I been spared the experience of it.

Amitabh introduced "themself" in the fullness of their identity, at last. And I came to a place of clarity, awe ...and peace ... with the reality of all that name represents. In my view, these teachings are a gift from a level of consciousness so profound as to defy description. You are free to believe, or disbelieve, that the source of these teachings is the aspect of God I believe them to be. And even though it is surely my privilege to share these teachings with you, I have no stake in having you share my perspective.

Your choices are your own. If these teachings feel like truth to you ...embrace them. And own them as your truth. That is the training. For "the calling" is an extraordinary, highly personal journey for each of us. As for me, what an incredible voyage it's been ...so far.

Rasha
June, 1997

THE
CALLING

PART I

1

You are about to embark upon a journey from which there is no return. For once you have heard and recognized the inner "calling"...the voice of silent knowingness that comes from the depths of one's own being ...and once you have chosen to honor that recognition of Divine truth and direct your life to follow it, your life will never be the same. This is an oftentimes frightening prospect for many who have heard "the calling." For they weigh within their minds a myriad mundane considerations. Whether they have really heard what they think they have heard; the implications inherent in following the life direction those inclinations imply; how much of the stake in the material world will have to be relinquished in order to follow a life path that is decidedly spiritual in focus; what others will think if they do ...and what they themselves will think, in retrospect, if they do not.

For those who have heard "the calling," the initial dilemma of how to proceed constitutes what has been termed a major "crisis in faith." For it presents to its recipient a crossroads of monumental proportions that requires, essentially, the relinquishing of all that is ego-based for the promise of the realization of the intangible. Coming from a material plane orientation, the prospect is fraught with risk. And, when colored by the limitation of judgment based on material values, sets off a chain reaction of self-confrontation. Confrontation with the very issues that would serve as impediments and stumbling blocks should "the calling" be taken up.

It is crucial that these issues be dealt with early in the process of 'becoming,' for if this aspect is not sufficiently explored within one's heart, the conflicts that will surface during the ever-intensifying process to come could render the individual incapable of functioning in any meaningful way on any level. For once the journey is embarked upon, there truly is no turning back ...not completely. For having once tasted of Divine truth, it will remain alive in your consciousness. And although you may certainly choose to turn your back upon your knowingness, and proceed with your earthly activities in pursuit of material rewards and mundane pleasures, you will not forget. You will never forget.

Many who have heard "the calling" choose to ignore its invitation out of fear. Others know that, in truth, it cannot be ignored. And though many proceed with great trepidation, they step bravely out upon the spiritual path, knowing that they have done so ...out of love. It is a choice that relatively few are given in these times. For most are not sufficiently developed as spiritual beings to undertake the challenges that such a step would require. For these ones, who constitute the masses now incarnate upon the earth plane, "the calling, "which is ever present, is inaudible. Yet, it re-echoes clearly in the hearts of others, who have responded to its cry instantly, in joyous, undeniable recognition of the elusive "something that was missing" all their lives. For most, however, the experience is neither black nor white. But hovers somewhere between the heart and the mind, between instinct and intellect, between the certainty of life as it is now known and a great, bright trail-without-end that is conspicuously devoid of signposts. And great battles ensue within these ones, as the agonizing process of "becoming" one who has recognized "the calling" begins.

It is somewhere within this nether world, which lies between accepted consensus reality and the true spiritual reality, that most who read these words now find themselves. For although many consider themselves to be truly on the Spiritual Path ...at least sometimes ...there are aspects of self that are still bound, by fear of the unknown, to the known, the familiar, the so-called "acceptable" codes of behavior and modes of belief. It is hoped that these teachings will help to bridge the gap for those who truly want to follow the Divine Spiritual Path and have prayed for the wisdom, the understanding, and the courage to let go of the restraints that they know are holding them back ...and to step onto the path with both feet.

There will be no guarantees. For those intent upon weighing the relative merits ...the potential 'risks' versus the 'rewards'...of such a choice, no clear-cut answers will be forthcoming. For the risks are too numerous to be counted, and the rewards are immeasurable. When placed in juxtaposition with what one knows beyond doubt that he has experienced within his heart, and what one knows he has felt emanating from his very own hands, it soon becomes clear that such considerations are irrelevant.

It takes more time for some than for others. But, without exception, "the calling," once heard, is unforgettable. For within it is a remembrance of things past. Not on a conscious level, but from an indefinable place of recognition that comes from within. And it forms a connection with who one truly is. A connection with countless lifetimes where "the calling" was heard. A connection with a deeper knowledge of why, perhaps, one chose to come into this particular lifetime, in this particular time frame.

7

A connection with a vast, new line of inner questions that, at last, appear to lead in a direction where real answers may be found.

The question arises frequently as to why, suddenly, life seems to have taken a radical turn in a direction that is, quite often, unexpected. Individuals leading what could be considered to be quite 'normal' lives suddenly encounter a teacher, a book, or a life-altering event of an experiential nature wherein a thought is re-awakened that had been waiting patiently, dormantly, for its appointed moment. Weeks, months, and even years transpire as the concept is assimilated and the full scope of the ramifications of that concept begin to truly formulate within one's consciousness. Ultimately, it is not possible to continue living as one had been, and relegate such a transformational realization to the passive role of a 'philosophy.' For the full realization of "the calling" calls for a radical turnabout in one's total approach to life and living. And requires that the awakening individual integrate spiritual awareness into action.

It is no longer possible to turn a blind eye to the limited, myopic parameters within which most of the present-day civilization operates. One becomes aware ...often painfully aware ... that the focus has shifted. And that the world and ones role in it is viewed very differently than it is by most with whom one still has day-to-day interaction. One begins to seek out like-minded individuals, and to avoid confrontation with the closed-mindedness with which one's newfound awareness is met on more traditional fronts. One learns discretion in determining with whom one shares new, intimate revelations. And with whom one, advisedly, does not. And in the recognition of the emerging family of like-minded individuals simultaneously undergoing this life-altering transformation is the comforting realization that YOU ARE NOT ALONE.

Know that when your heart has opened in earnest to the acceptance of Divine Truth as your own truth, it is not possible, in any conscience, to continue enacting and embodying cultural conditioning. The conflicts and doubts that arise in the realization of this fact are an expected part of the process. Know that there will be bouts of confusion, depression, and denial. There will be intellectualization and rationalization of rudimentary understandings that precede their deeper integration within. It is a gradual, ongoing process that takes many stages of development to achieve. One does not simply flip a switch, when the 'Light goes on,' and experience instant enlightenment. Expect that there will be setbacks ...and quantum leaps. There will be moments of ecstatic elation and utter despair, as the full realization of "the calling" and all it implies takes root. For this understanding is the culmination of countless lifetimes of preparation for the perfect moment for the manifestation of that understanding in your physical reality.

There is a sense that the lens of limitation through which one had been accustomed to viewing the world has altered. And that a clearer focus is now possible. One's perceptions and sensings are suddenly more acute. And there is an impeccable logic to all of it, where once only chaos reigned. And amidst the joy and the sadness that one often experiences simultaneously when "the calling" hits home; amidst the sense of a beginning and an ending; amidst the feeling of having died and having suddenly been born; there is, at last, an answer. A rationale for all of it. And an undeniable sense of a perfection in it that could only be Divine.

Listen carefully to "the calling" of your heart. For within it is the voice of God, telling you, at last, it's time. Time to become who you really are. Time to rise above the masses of festering humanity and attain a rarefied perspective. Time to relinquish the limitations fostered by fear, and embrace the truth that is conceived in love.

"The calling" has summoned you to these pages. And to the series of progressive, developmental stages that preceded this moment and paved the way for your assimilation of that higher

octave of understanding. It is with a focus upon the dynamics
of that process of initial spiritual 'breakthrough' ...the refinement
of the understandings underlying the process of 'becoming' ...
that we embark upon this journey of exploration, together.

2

Each one on the Divine Path begins awakening to the true nature of reality in much the same way. The process starts with a growing awareness of the uncanny perfection of the world of nature. A sense of wonder begins to permeate the consciousness, and the ultimate question "How can this be so?" becomes undeniable. Deep within, a dormant seed of knowingness begins to sprout, and the roots of that concept grasp lovingly the fertile soil of the heart that seeks to reunite with the love of the Creator. The sense that there is more to reality than meets the eye is integrated into conscious awareness. And the quantum leap between believing and knowing to your very depths that Divinity is at work here on earth ...is achieved.

That is the barest beginning of what has come to be termed "enlightenment." And for most of humanity, the process ends here, if begun at all. For some, however, this stage of spiritual growth is the stepping stone to the opening of heightened awareness and the ability to vibrate to the higher octaves of Light energy. Ultimately, when such a process is carried to fruition, the individual is able to transcend physical limitation and become one with his highest expression of self, as an aspect of that Divinity. The ability to bridge the gap between the physical state and the altered states of higher consciousness is becoming more and more prevalent, as those who have made a soul choice to assist in the transformation of the planet in this lifetime come into the fullness of their potential as expressions of Light energy in human, physical form.

Such individuals, by now, have sought some expression of that knowingness. And most are serving the Light in some capacity, often without fully knowing or understanding why. Complete rational understanding is not a prerequisite for full, devoted participation in the mission before us now. All that is required is merely a willingness to become all that one is capable of becoming, and a willingness to integrate the fullness of the Light energy into one's totality. It is not enough to regard oneself as a limited physical creature who has chosen to lend one's hands, in one's spare time, as a 'wire' through which Divine Light is permitted to pass. The highest expression of humanness is in integrating Godliness into one's being, so that in the transference of the Light energy, one actually becomes one with the energy ...one IS the Light. And that state of conscious awareness is critical in maximizing the potential for each to elevate his own vibration to the extent that one is able to transcend the physical and embody the physical simultaneously.

Each individual rising to the ultimate expression of humanness in this lifetime has the potential for becoming God-like in physical form ...a human expression of Divine knowledge, wisdom, and love. It is not necessary to regard the physical state as a limitation in the times at hand. For Divine capabilities are being placed in the hands of the willing and most able. Each carries within his spiritual genetic coding the potential for embodying all the inherent 'miraculous' abilities heretofore reserved for avatars. What has come to be termed Christ consciousness is the condition that all souls who survive into the Great Spiritual Age will attain. For in the coming times, none will remain who are defined by the limitation of physical expression. The beings of the Age of Spirit will be spiritual beings who have access to physical form for its useful aspects, but are not bound by physical self-definition.

A normal state of being will incorporate all aspects of physical beingness with the unlimited condition of elevated souls on other planes of existence. It will be possible for interdimensional travel and experience, without relinquishing form. There are many who presently have cultivated the ability to travel to other dimensions and experience those conditions at a spirit level. Many have developed the ability to "astral travel" in a conscious state, and/or are aware that such interdimensional experience is an integral part of what is termed "dream state." In the deepest levels of sleep, all human souls depart the physical body and journey to other planes of experience to replenish the spiritual self. It is for this reason that detrimental effects are experienced when sleep deprivation occurs. It is not for reasons of physical 'rest' but for reasons of spiritual nourishment that sleep occurs. For it is during these periods ...often with a duration of mere minutes or seconds in linear measurement terms ...that an individual reunites with the 'all-knowing' highest aspect of self and surmounts the limitation of incarnate personality.

In the coming times, that state of being will become standard for all who choose to remain in physical form. If the life lessons are learned and completion of the birth/death cycle is achieved, it is entirely possible for those to ascend with the physical body, when physical transition ultimately occurs. This is the supreme expression of humanness and is the epitome of the possibilities attainable in this lifetime. It is a rarefied state, reserved for those who rise above the ranks that divide men and become one with all Creation. It is a state that many who will serve in leadership roles in the times to come can hope and expect to achieve. It is the goal toward which all who rise to the true challenge of these times are striving ...whether they are consciously aware of it or not.

This is the fundamental reason for emphasis on the condition of the physical body in the coming times. For it is with this one physical expression of humanness that the ascending being will travel beyond the physical. And this form will endure thereafter ...for eternity. Care well for the physical form you inhabit in this moment and in every moment. Honor the physical body and preserve its sanctity by making every effort to purify and detoxify it. For within the physical make-up of this incarnate identity will reside the sum total of one's countless incarnations, the totality of one's knowingness, the full expression of each individual's capacity to embody the God-force and all it represents.

Guard well the precious seed of life with which you have been entrusted. For its condition will contribute toward determining the level you will be able to attain in the times to come. The composite it represents, in the final analysis, will reflect the consummate vibration of the individual residing therein. And at the same time, the vibration attained will be affected directly by the condition of the physical form. It is a system conceived in balance, in which you have full control over the potential that was your birthright in coming into this lifetime.

Heed well this message, for it is perhaps the single most important concept upon which you may choose to focus in the immediate present. The attainment of spiritual elevation is an ongoing process that evolves over one's entire physical lifetime. It is not a condition suddenly arrived upon, but one that is perpetually unfolding. As one's awareness expands, drawing one ever nearer to oneness with Divinity, the individual comes to embody the universe itself ... ever expanding and growing to encompass a state that is conceived in limitlessness. It is a process that has neither beginning nor ending, but is the essence of the eternal.

The moment in time in which you now find yourself reflects merely a poignant pause in an ever-ongoing momentum. It provides the space to bring into conscious awareness a major crossroads in your soul development, and to embody that spark of understanding into every expression, in every action, in every cell of one's being. Do not expect that the process ends at any given point, where having completed a given course of study, you are tested, graded, and given a diploma ...as a laurel upon which you can rest forevermore. It is not that simple. For even the great masters ...the very wisest of beings who passed through the physical plane and in the lifetimes of greatest significance left an indelible mark on humanity ...continue to grow from the dimensions of spirit, in their individual embodiments of oneness with all Creation. In this moment ...in any given moment ...all one can do is maximize that moment. And in this moment, you are in physical form ...bound by it, defined by it, honored by it, or limited by it ...the choices are yours to make.

Concern yourself not so much with aspects of selfhood that are destined to take eons to attain full expression, but focus upon the aspect of self expressed in the now. Hone and finetune that form ...with eternal gratitude that you have been blessed with the opportunity to do so. Other aspects are equally able to be cultivated in other dimensions. The opportunity of physical incarnation was chosen by you who read these words for good reason. It is for advantages of experience that is measurable that you have come, in order to leave that arena and carry that attainment into the realm of the immeasurable.

Time, in all its limitation as a linear illusion, affords an individual the luxury of being able to isolate and identify key points in one's growth. It is for this, amongst many reasons, that physical form was chosen as the optimum opportunity for growth at this point in your personal development. Utilize well this 'time' to perfect the physical representation of your beingness. Train and nourish the body well, cleanse it constantly, and sanctify it with constant exposure to Divine Light energy so that it may flourish with unlimited vitality, and carry the life force within to the Spirit world of tomorrow ...and to the world of Spirit, where perhaps you now travel only in your dreams.

For beyond the 'tomorrowland' destined to blossom upon the earth plane lies the timeless realm of oneness with the God-force, to which you have been extended a tentative invitation. The RSVP is a never-ending decision, made and remade with every nuance of every waking moment. It is an invitation you carry with you at all times, engraved in the structure of your spiritual genetic code and printed out beautifully in every cell of your physical being. Blessed is he who honors and recognizes self as a boundless expression of that knowingness, and never questions that he is eminently worthy of the distinction ...with humblest gratitude that this is so.

Hold your head high in self-acknowledgment of your blossoming awareness, and be not seduced into debasing your vibration in well-meant expressions of self-effacement. Humility of the heart does not presuppose humbling oneself, necessarily, before any man ...but before God alone. Subject yourself not to the judgment of men, however well meaning, if that judgment serves to injure and debase, disproportionate to the elevation possible in the potential lesson to be learned. For the tendency is commonplace amongst those who have set out on this quest of spirit, to kneel down before the altar of criticism. Just because a pill is bitter, doesn't constitute proof that it is potentially beneficial. This only you can judge for yourself. And judgment, in itself, is best reserved FOR the self. Ultimately, until you answer directly to the Creator, your own judgment supersedes any that may be thrust upon you, regardless of whether some other self-elevated being has determined that the lessons are his to dispense.

Do not be deceived into believing that life lessons are forthcoming from anything but actual life experience ...the lesson lying in your own ability to grasp the potential growth within that experience. Do not be so eager to humble yourself before those who have set themselves up in judgment of spiritual seekers. For, too often, the very lessons they attempt to impart are those upon which they themselves most need to focus. And lost in the delusion that they have been placed here to weigh the spiritual merits of others traveling on the path, and to dispense self-created spiritual medication, have lost sight of the fact that each encounter is merely a life experience for THEM, to help mirror effort that should be directed within.

Do not be tempted to fall into this trap. For as you rise in vibration and in enlightened consciousness, others will look to YOU for answers; to tell them where they are wandering astray; to identify FOR them their self-perceived failings. To be lured into doing so is to lose sight of one's own prime focus, and to deprive another of the rich potential in the experience of developing discernment.

Each is on his own timetable. And it is not for any who read these words to assume that he is in a position to provide judgmental insights for another. Rather, it is the true teacher who gives clues from the sharing of his own life experience and leaves it to the intuitive powers of the recipient to apply these insights to his own situation, and incorporate that pearl of life experience into the script that he writes in every ongoing moment. Do not attempt to do another's thinking FOR them, but turn the question back upon the student for exploration within the inner reaches of the consciousness, where real growth occurs. For, when grasped merely on an intellectual level, true understanding is forfeited and the opportunity for significant spiritual advancement lost. The greatest learning comes from within the deepest reaches of the individual soul. For in the eyes of one's own heart is the only mirror of the soul that provides a reflection worth regarding. Look at it. And smile. Often.

3

In the beginning, man was a God-centered being, focused in his knowledge that he was an expression of the Creator's intention to establish, in this physical realm, a representation of His presence. The peace and harmony that are the essence of Divine vibration were instilled within each and every creature, human and non-human. And a loving air of selfless participation in helping to co-create the expression of that intention permeated the consciousness of all.

There was no thought in those times to bettering one's lot, nor to outshining others. There was no tendency toward viewing the intentions of others as anything less than the purity that all knew, to their very depths, was their own. There was never a thought to aspiring to the achievements of others, nor to the material rewards that accompanied them. There was no thought of doing less than the ultimate expression of one's own God-given capabilities. It was a realm in which all gave their all for the mutual benefit of all. And none perceived a sense of separation of purpose from another, nor from the totality that was Divine. It was in this harmonious environment that man was to dwell. And it is to this expression of spirit-centered perfection and oneness with all Creation that he is destined to return.

Every major religion, throughout your earth-plane history has documented what has come to be known as man's fall from grace. And there has emerged, over time, a vast body of contradictory information that would explain and rationalize the reasons underlying man's divergence from his spiritually-centered beginnings. There is much truth and much distortion in most of it. Man's need to "know" began the process that ultimately led to his obscuring of the Divine focus with which he was created. The need to know the essence of his own nature. The need to understand the mechanics of his existence. The need to reach out and harness what he perceived to be the vehicle for becoming Divine. Each, within himself, began to reach beyond blanket acceptance of his oneness with the totality ...to become "more." And in the sense of separation man created for himself in that striving came the concept of EGO. Man was no longer satisfied with harmonization. He no longer viewed his existence as an opportunity that was focused in the experiential ...a chance to taste, in his physical expression, the perfection in unity. He wanted more. And in that concept of more, man created the downward spiral upon which he has perpetuated his striving to improve upon perfection.

As the separation amongst men came to be perceived within the consciousness of each, each in his search for the key to limitlessness created his own limitations. For the concept of limitation, by definition, could only exist relative to someone or something else. And in the fragmentation of the initial unity of purpose, man emerged with a minute expression of what he once was able to experience in the totality. Given that diminished capacity and that diminished vibration, he sought through intellectual means to re-create his remembrance of what he had understood to be his own essence. But that state-of-being could not come to be, under conditions of self-perceived "separation."

Eventually, even the remembrance was lost. All that remained was the concept of "striving" and the concept of differentiation from all else that was once a united Creation. Man forgot that, initially, the striving was toward improving upon the perfection of a God-centered existence. He forgot that peace and harmony were the foundations of the world in which he now perceived himself to be lost. He saw himself as isolated within his identity. And in that space of isolation he created "fear." He no longer knew, unquestioningly, that all were there in harmony for the glory of all. He, in his aloneness, came to perceive the need to focus his attentions on his own physical well-being and survival. Others, who were also focused only on their own physical survival were seen as a potential threat. And walls were erected mentally that reinforced the perception of separation from the ONENESS that escalated exponentially.

Existance became rooted in fear for one's safety and survival. The concept of immortality and the unquestioned understanding that physical existence was but a limited expression of an essence that could not be destroyed ...with which man was initially instilled ...became lost. Man came to perceive the physical expression of his beingness as "all there is," and fortified his abilities to preserve it at all costs. His entire focus turned to his own physical survival, and it became his only reason for being.

One's connection with the Creator and the part that each played as a harmonizing aspect of Creation became totally obscured in the clouds of negative karma man began to accumulate in his strivings for MATERIAL elevation. For to be "above," there had, by definition, to be something or someone "below." And in that effort to outdo and outshine, it came to be perceived as less important if harm came to another, as long as one remained "ahead." Life became a race without a goal ...striving for the sake of striving. And the only purpose to one's existence came to be the accumulation of material evidence of a sense of self-worth based on a foundation of fear of unworthiness. One focused all one's efforts on amassing physical proof of one's elevation, irregardless of the detriment incurred by others individually and by humankind as a whole. Those who found themselves trailing in this race compromised their integrity to gain an 'edge,' and escalated the amount of negative karma with which they became increasingly burdened.

With the accumulating weight of negative karma under which man began to stagger came the relative diminishing of his spiritual vibration and the inclination to focus his energies in activities that would perpetuate that ongoing condition. He used his free will exclusively for his own material betterment. And in time, free will came into karmic balance with the cause-and-effect laws upon which the universe is based. Man seemed to be no longer automatically able to create his reality, but increasingly came to perceive himself as the "victim" of events and circumstances he could not control.

Negative emotions arose within him, as the perceived injustice was met by retaliation, which only served to create more negative karma. This, in turn, created more "negative" occurrences through which that karma could be counterbalanced. Clans bonded together to unite their efforts toward over-powering other clans. Group karma resulted, as nations rose up to dominate and subjugate other nations, and to create material expressions of that powerbase that would come to threaten the well-being of the planet itself. The collective vibration upon the earth became so dense, so dark, and so charged with negativity that the isolated sparks of Light ...the rare ones whose hearts could see beyond the limitations of physical reality, to a Divinity and a logic that superseded materialism ...were all but obscured.

Through intensive karmic compensation over the centuries, some have emerged, in these times, with a relative clarity of vision that could lead back to the Source, if cultivated with care. These ones have begun to recognize the atrocity that is your physical dimension. And they speak out, with varying degrees of conviction, and share their vision ...their concept of a reality for which there is yet to be substantial material evidence. They oftentimes do not know where they derive these concepts, only that somewhere within the core of their beings they recognize them as truth. In that recognition, the Light from within these ones begins to shine a bit brighter. And it is recognized by others, just on the brink of that breakthrough and the reversal of their own participation and unquestioning acceptance of the collective falsehood that constitutes your consensus reality. And the flicker of Light grows a little bit brighter.

As, one by one, these flames of recognition are rekindled within the consciousness of each of you who dare to embrace the Light and the truth ...however unpopular that stance may be ...the Light grows a little bit brighter. And suddenly, for these ones, there is a purpose. There is a logic. There is a vision. And they remember. Not consciously. But the SENSE of the ancient memories are rekindled. And with them, a bond is re-established with one's own Divine essence.

It is this renewed sense of connectedness with one's own Divinity, and one's personal connection with the Creator, that provides the momentum for the grueling process of transformation so many are undergoing in these times. Once the connection is re-established in one's conscious awareness, the process becomes that of weeding out and releasing the programmed conditioning that would have you deny the truth in that connectedness.

Ultimately, there are no doubts. There are no limitations. There is no reluctance. And there is no question that the intensive search for the 'meaning' of one's existence which has taken untold thousands of years, has come full circle. When you have reached that realization, you become ONE with that realization.

And ONE with a legion of awakened souls, who together will re-establish the perfection in the beginnings from whence you've come.

4

Never before in man's history on this planet has there been an opportunity such as this one for ultimate karmic resolution and the reversal, in totality, of the adverse direction which humankind has chosen. These are times of completion, and of confrontation with the distortions that constitute your physical plane reality and your understandings of its nature.

As the clock races with undeterred determination toward a rendezvous with a destiny that is inevitable, those of you who have been permitted to play a part in this important period in history are caught in the grip of conflicting energies. It is these powerful forces that create, within the consciousness of those capable of perceiving, a sense of alternately backsliding and sprinting ahead upon the path. Those who remain tethered by circumstance to material plane obligations often feel as though there were a virtual tug of war transpiring within. As though something or someone was vying, within the very depths of one's being, for the authority to determine an ultimate life direction that one seems unable to envision.

The spiritual focus of one's life remains in the realm of 'instinct' and defies rationale. But there one stands, as if bound, nevertheless. And there one will remain, indefinitely if necessary, until it is recognized and thoroughly acknowledged that these times require a total focus of energy and intention. In order to truly be of service, it is necessary to virtually 'dissect' oneself out of one's previous life script ...and place the reins in the hands of God. The lesson here is FAITH. And trust in the knowledge that the direction in which one's knowingness is navigating one's life IS viable ...even if, for the moment yet, it remains invisible.

For those of you still caught in the living 'limbo' of uncertainty that characterizes the timeless space of this transitional period, the obstacles to 'success' as you may have known it in material plane terms become ever more formidable. You question how you will be capable of maintaining physical sustenance while simultaneously disconnecting yourself from its source. Alternative possibilities elude you. Everywhere you turn is perceived a 'dead end' which would lead you back from whence you came, and not in the direction in which you perceive yourself to be headed.

All the while, you cling to the old structure as a safety raft, not daring to venture forth, not daring to believe that solid ground looms just over the horizon, obscured only by vision that continues to cling to what is known, familiar, and provable. And until you are able to rally the courage to release your grip on that so-called security, there you will remain, unable to create the possibilities that would constitute the foundations of a new direction. It is only by truly letting go of the one, that you are able to realize the other. And much precious time is being wasted by many who deliberate endlessly over whether or not it is 'safe' to venture forth into uncharted territory. For to do so defies logic ...defies the very premises upon which your experience upon this planet is based. And yet it IS that very concept ...physical plane 'logic' ... which has you bound to a blindness to anything more.

It is for you now lost in that uncertainty; those of you still frozen into inaction by a fear of acting incorrectly; those of you whose lives hover in a perpetual state of suspended animation, to understand clearly the cause of that condition. And to determine whether you are willing to commit yourself totally. Whether you have the courage to act on your instincts rather than your logical capabilities. Whether you are capable of taking a 'blind leap of faith' in these times, knowing that either way your very life is at stake.

This is the barrier that must be dealt with now, if there is to be any possibility of a 'future' as you would perceive it. For the times now upon us require a fortitude and a focus of intention. It requires a level of trust in one's own abilities to perceive and to 'source' information that would provide a sense of direction wherein there is no question, there is no doubt, there is no room for anything but God-focused clarity ... decisiveness that comes of knowing that your inner-directedness is in alignment with your own highest purpose. This is the state of being to which you aspire, at the deepest level. And though you may not be in full conscious awareness of the state toward which you are being propelled at a soul level, that lack of conscious clarity does not serve to negate the fact that you are moving ...albeit, perhaps even in spite of yourself ...in that direction.

The need to perpetually analyze and assess one's current 'status' heralds little more than an acute awareness of one's own self-perceived lack of progress. For the growth of which we speak is not measurable in linear terms and is not necessarily indicated by the external evidence provided by current life circumstances. Your ability to confront those circumstances, and the havoc you may perceive to be what WAS your life, is more an indication of progress in a positive direction than otherwise. Were things to remain the same ...with a continued focus on material 'success' to the exclusion of all else ...you could correctly assume that progress was NOT being made. The very fact that your circumstances may appear chaotic, that your life has lost any recognizable sense of direction, that you look wistfully back upon what you regard as moments of clarity that now elude you ...all are indicative of the state of transition that is a necessary stage in the process of true spiritual awakening.

There is no easy route to the ultimate destination toward which you travel. The journey is made step by step. Painstakingly. It is for you who find yourselves in the moments of greatest despair, to let go of the fears that bind you to a need for the familiar, and to trust that the way will remain unclear until you are able to do so. All who have traveled this path in physical form since time immemorial have confronted and transcended the need to be tethered to consensus reality. All who aspire to advancing beyond that limitation must be willing, unconditionally, to make a commitment to action based upon inner-knowingness, rather than upon linear logic.

It is not enough to have intellectually accepted certain realizations. For leadership in these times is not about intellectualization ...but about action. It is about having the courage to act upon one's inner convictions, even when that stance is in opposition to public opinion. For the general public is not destined in the direction in which you may well be headed. Many will succumb to their own stubborn refusal to concede that there is anything more to reality than meets the eye. They will have sought the 'safety' in the scientifically provable, and collided with conditions based not in conventional wisdom but in the inevitability of Divine Wisdom.

For those whose spiritual destiny it is to be candidates for transformation, present times represent preparation. Take the time now to focus upon the changes occurring within your very essence, and allow those changes to manifest into decisive clarity of action that reflects not one's expectations ...but one's freedom from them. By allowing the universe to provide for you precisely the right circumstances for your optimum participation in these times, you will have taken a giant step upon the path. And will have allowed your own destiny the opportunity to unfold, in ways you may never have dreamed.

Once you are willing to express your faith by acting upon your instincts ...rather than dissecting them, analyzing them, and hedging your bets by testing them out in relation to what may or may not be scientifically verifiable ...you will have passed the crucial milestone beyond which clouds of uncertainty no longer obscure your vision of what is possible. It is toward confrontation with this turning point that we encourage you to strive in the present. So that you may know the wonders that loom upon the horizon ...just around the bend.

5

From the beginning, there was a master plan set down by the Creator, which established within a given time frame certain progressive steps through which humanity was to move in order to rise to a certain level of spiritual purification. Many incarnations were permitted each soul, so that a rich breadth of life experiences could mesh with wisdom and knowingness gained in astral 'lifetimes,' enabling the soul to emerge, toward the end of the cycle of birth and death, with an unquestioning sense of oneness with The Creator and with all expressions of what you would term "life." Such a point has been reached by relatively few in your earthbound history. Many have proved themselves to be unworthy of incarnations that would significantly advance those souls, and concentrate primarily on the working out of simple, primitive instincts, and the exploring of levels of ego at the most rudimentary levels.

Relatively few have been privileged to glimpse the possibility that there exists, beyond the realm of your physical reality, a profound purpose, a meticulous logic, and a glory of spiritual expression that supersedes anything known in physical form. It is with these select few individuals, numbering perhaps in the tens of thousands currently incarnate today, that the focus of our interest lies. For it is in these precious pioneers that the seeds of the coming Spiritual Civilization have been implanted. Those who have been 'tapped' in this way are coming ...some quite suddenly ...into spiritual 'awareness.' And a compelling urgency to reach beyond the mundane toward the metaphysical becomes an undeniable, major theme in those lives. It is not coincidence that these individuals are thus driven to re-prioritize their lives. For they are being guided, most carefully and specifically, so that they are in a state of preparedness and accepting of circumstances which are likely to arise.

Such preparedness is built on a foundation of detachment from the emotional constraints of the life/death transition. Freedom from fear of this momentary crossing-over is a rudimentary prerequisite for functioning at even the most basic level in the times to come. For the transitions will be massive, sudden, and monumental. The ability to deal with the spiritual elevation of the living, primarily the very young, to ease the trauma that will inevitably accompany events to come, is imperative. The fact of death will become a routine fact of life, as the majority of souls currently incarnate will choose either to pre-empt the coming times, or to make their transition en masse with the bulk of humanity. Those whose destiny it is to remain physically incarnate on this planet will need to have a deep-seated understanding that this turn of events is not an ending, but rather a beginning. A fresh start of historic significance.

It is important, at a very young age, that children be taught the reality of the birth/death cycle ...that which you would term "reincarnation." That way, in the face of what is to come, they can proceed with courage and with a sense of moving forward, rather than viewing those circumstances as an insurmountable defeat of the human species. This lifetime is, for them, the ultimate test of all the qualities that they have brought forth from thousands of years of trial and error. This lifetime is, for them, the one in which they will truly "make a difference." Not in terms of personal posterity, which is based in ego, but in terms of acting in oneness with all fellow creatures …with all fellow humans. The outcome is one in which none needs to outshine others. A state in which all are truly equal, pulling in oneness for the Divine glory and the united exultation of all.

It is a radical deviation from the instinctive course of human beings …what you would term "human nature" …which is centered upon one's differentiation from one's fellow creatures and from one's fellow men. Striving for individual gain or individual distinction is based entirely upon the needs of ego. It is time now to rise above these baser instincts. For your individual history is not carved in the relatively fragile stone of this physical plane, but carved upon the indestructible soul within each.

It is the deeds done and the intentions with which they are accomplished that would determine true 'merit,' if any, in a given lifetime. It matters not whether fame and fortune are achieved as a result of these actions. There is no higher 'rank' allotted those whose lifetime was more fortunate and well compensated than another's. But rather, the true 'rank' would be assigned after the chapter is completed. And it surprises many to discover, once on the other side, that all their so-called 'accomplishments' count for little indeed, in the truest sense. It may well be the pauper with the selfless 'heart of gold' that rises to the head of the class, as it were. And the clever billionaire whose life was the embodiment of deceit and trickery, who is, in the final analysis, a 'failure' in the life lessons to have been learned.

It matters not in which profession one chooses to express his talents. It matters not in which country one lives, the color of one's skin or which religion one professes to practice. What matters are the simple, day-to-day interactions with one's fellowmen. Instruct well the young. Not in how to 'succeed,' but in how to deal with fairness and compassion in every human encounter. Not in how to best express taste and style, for the purpose of outshining others, but for the purpose of improving the condition of living and the quality of the time spent here, for all.

There was, as you know, one recent, abysmal attempt at mass egolessness in your history ....known as communism. As a concept it was distorted and used as a way to repress many for the glory of few. Side by side with the more material-based cultures, the way of communism came to be viewed by those under its control, as a means of crushing the human spirit. And indeed, that was the result, in most cases. Taken in the way the concept was intended, however, when implanted within the consciousness of those in the position of leadership ...IF COMBINED WITH A STRONG, LOVING SENSE OF DIVINE PARTICIPA-TION AND PURPOSE ...it could have emerged as a power-ful, positive step forward for mankind.

The misdirection was in taking the concept of "oneness" in only the material sense, and thus distorting and tying the hands of a concept with a potentially infinite reach. The absence of the God-presence in the idea relegated the entire episode as an aborted chapter in what was to have been an advancing chronicle in human evolution. It is not surprising that those suppressed under those regimes have arisen to surmount the restrictions imposed. For there was no lesson, in the deepest sense, to be learned in the continued adherence to this way of life. In future times, the real meaning of that experiment will 'come to light.' For when man does, indeed, 'come into the Light,' all will be illuminated. And the need for differentiation amongst men will be a mere particle in what will become ancient history.

Those among you who will lead the human race into the coming age are already one, in spirit, with the Divine purpose and the Divine Plan. You are harbingers of a higher truth, reaching out with the fingers of God to touch and to be touched by those with whom you share the sacred knowingness of God's infinite love …for all creatures.

6

WHEN the realization is integrated into conscious awareness that reality as most know it, is but a fragmentary glimpse of true reality, the process of awakening is permitted to begin in earnest. Those who are experiencing this phenomenon as a frequent recurrence are apt, at first, to dismiss such thoughts or perceptions as accidental slips of the imagination. When the thought pattern becomes undeniable, the individual realizes it is indeed time for making conscious choices as to whether or not one can continue to subscribe to a system of consensus reality or whether it is time to risk the possibility that one may either be insane or capable of a more profound perception of the phenomenon referred to as life.

It is soon apparent that there is little real choice in this, for one's own knowingness will not let rest that which one's own experience has proved to be so. Recognizing and following that truth further reinforces the beliefs one has come to embrace. And it is a natural by-product of this developmental process to feel distanced from certain individuals with whom one formerly felt connected. In fact, this phenomenon escalates to the extent that one realizes that he has distanced himself from virtually every connection, both interpersonal and philosophical, that formerly gave his life definition and structure. It becomes necessary, ultimately, to relinquish those limitations and to sever the ties that bind one to a path that is no longer applicable or relevant to life in its evolving form.

The pattern is predictable. Yet, when it occurs, it is likely that the person will internalize the experience and personalize its effects. It is likely that one will perceive a profound sense of loss, and it will seem as if life has become an unending series of endings, unaccompanied by the corresponding sense of 'beginnings' that will follow. The two aspects of the process do not occur simultaneously, as one might expect. But rather that one aspect of the process lays the foundation for the building of a solid concept upon which to base one's newfound awareness. Much as when constructing a building, the ground must be cleared, old structures must be removed, carted away, and the area smoothed over to make preparation for a new structure that will stand fresh and firmly constructed in its place. The new structure does not emerge in its entirety on day one. But is formed, brick by brick, layer after layer, each level dependent upon the solidity, or lack thereof, of the layer upon which it rests. If care is taken with every stage of the new construction, the resulting structure has an excellent chance of standing and serving the purpose for which it was intended.

The analogy is obvious and extremely apt to the developmental process in the evolution of coming into what is termed "enlightenment." Sometimes the dismantling of the old structure is accompanied by deep feelings of emptiness and rootlessness. And one experiences a sentimental attachment to the old, often simply because it is familiar. At this stage, one most probably has not yet developed the vision necessary to foresee the structure that lies ahead, or have a concept of the use to which the leveled site will be put. But the fact that demolition crews have been called in is undeniable. And though a tear may be shed in the process of 'clearing out,' the accompanying emotion does not dispel the reality of what is transpiring, or the deep-seated feeling that this stage of one's life is inevitable and the process is one of long-term benefit and significance.

Once the ground is cleared and construction begins in earnest, the twinges of nostalgia for the old structure diminish, and fade into the haze of the broad category one comes to regard as one's 'previous life.' As if the sum totality of one's life experiences up to the transformational phase were encapsulated into a separate lifetime, and that somehow one has indeed been 'born again.' But in order for that birth into the fullness of one's awareness to occur, a 'death' of the old is necessary.

It is in this state of 'dying' that many coming into full aware-ness in these times find themselves. While the process is ongo-ing, one is likely to experience all of the emotional accompani-ments of the death experience. A sense of finality and a time of mourning are quite common and very appropriate reactions. And although it is certainly possible to make the transition with-out running oneself through the full gamut of emotional tur-moil, this cool-headed handling of the transformative experi-ence is rare. Most experience the process as a series of giant steps interspersed with occasional emotional setbacks and grave doubts regarding the radical turn in the direction of one's life. The negative feedback that so frequently accompanies this pro-cess, on the part of close family members and so-called friends, only serves to foster doubt and prolong the agony. Ultimately, one realizes that one has the choice of basing one's beliefs on one's own perceptions of reality or upon the oftentimes vocifer-ous consensus thinking of which one feels less and less a part as the days go by.

It is not a path of no return, for the most part. One can reverse the trend and cling to the old structure at any given time. And one is then left with the half-dismantled ruins of a structure that has ceased to be recognizable. This realization serves to help the individual see that there is, in the truest sense, no 'going back.' Though technically, one could deviate from the blueprint and call off the wrecking crew at any moment one chooses. It is somehow not the same. One comes to face the obvious truth that for him, the concept of loss is inevitable, either way. A sense of resolve overrides the reluctance to part with things past. And one's life is ready to proceed according to plan. The length of time it takes an individual to accomplish the transitional period varies with each individual, and may take weeks, months, or even years, until the stage where there is no longer resistance to the acceptance of truth as perceived, rather than 'truth' as believed.

It is in this virtual 'no-man's-land' between the death and subsequent rebirth that so many Light workers find themselves in the present times. Each, somehow, truly believes he is alone in these experiences. And feels victimized by the changes that are occurring ...albeit, often by choice. The lesson here for those caught in the throes of enlightenment transition is self-trust. Trusting one's inner knowingness against all odds, despite all resistance from others, irrespective of the 'price' in material terms that one may have to pay for the privilege. For the result is truly priceless. And though one often experiences the sense of the unknown in the pit of one's stomach, there is also the feeling that somehow it will all work out. There comes the point that one has invested so much in terms of loss, and in terms of the consequences of following one's heart, that the individual knows there is really nothing to lose by relinquishing all constraints. In essence, at that point, a commitment to the new life direction is made and reconstruction can then begin.

Fear not that you ...each of you undergoing this experience ...are alone in this. For unbeknownst to you, many are having the identical experience, in terms of life lesson integration, with varying degrees of discomfort. In the final analysis, each of you will step forward in his newfound skin and realize that a metamorphosis has taken place. And that what was really there, underlying it all that time, is you. The real one. Stripped of all the false trappings of a lifetime in which partial truth was the only truth. And one sees the safety in the freedom, rather than the safety in the security of the familiar. For the safety that once was, is indeed a self-limiting trap that is no longer necessary.

The trust and love of self become the foundation on which you are then permitted to begin building. And upon that foundation, there is no limit to what can be designed or achieved, if one has the will to do so. Material loss is often followed by unexpected material gain. Loss of love is replaced by love of self, and oftentimes the forming of deep, meaningful bonds of spirit with others of similar experience, surprisingly and happily. The sense of satisfaction is virtually guaranteed, if one only has the courage to follow the process through to its logical and inevitable conclusion. And though you may not yet see it from the perspective from which you view the radical events in your life in these times, the view of the path ahead will be crystal clear, bright, and uncluttered with the brambles of self-doubt, sooner than you may now expect.

Have the courage to act on your own inner convictions. And reach beyond the mundane. For a world of wonder awaits you when resistance to change is replaced by a willingness to embrace yourself, at long last, for the messenger of Love that you really are.

7

THE obligation one assumes in setting forth upon a spiritual path is ultimately to oneself. You may delude yourself into believing that you have sacrificed self for an altruistic higher purpose, and that may indeed be the result of your efforts. But the true underlying purpose is the elevation of self and the embodiment of the principles set down by the Creator. It is only through true self-mastery that one is able to serve the broader spectrum, and be of service to mankind. Self-sacrifice is not the objective here, but rather, self-knowledge. Self-perceived, altruistic motives alone for devotion of one's time and energies to the service of The Light are, in truth, counterproductive to the long term objective of this interdimensional effort ...which is the elevation of each soul to the ultimate level individually possible. You may devote yourself to the service of others, but know that in so doing you serve the best interests of your own soul-self and, in this way, are of the highest possible service to God.

Each soul is an investment of the God energy. A potential unrealized. A seed with all the capabilities of sprouting, rooting, flowering, and bearing fruit whose seeds will themselves carry that potential. The process is ongoing and never-ending. And will carry you to the heights of human experience, if cultivated with loving care. Seated deep within the heart must be the all-pervading awareness of the role the God energy plays in every aspect of the process. Crediting oneself with the progress made, is in essence nullifying the 'charge' that the achievement carries. Thus, the physical embodiment might be achieved, and yet the point of the exercise missed entirely, unless full awareness is directed toward the concept of GRATITUDE.

It is the humbled heart that is most open to the voice of the Creator. And it is the voice of gratitude for ALL things that is the most readily heard. Every breath you are permitted to take is only by Divine sanction. Every bounty that you reap is only the result of God's allowing it to be so. Self-responsibility, thus, is a concept held in the delicate balance between self-directed action and results that are manifested by the grace of God.

The notion popularly accepted that one determines one's own reality and creates the events that play in the drama of one's life is a pseudo-truth. One magnetizes energies and the resulting manifestations of those energies by one's choices and the actions taken upon them. Yet, what is all too often overlooked is the role of Divine responsibility in guiding those actions so that the optimum life lessons are provided for each individual in every moment. It is all well and good to wish upon stars, request Divine intervention, and plot one's course in the physical realm with clever strategy ...and those actions can manifest some level of results. But the outcome is limited unless those actions are accompanied by the understanding within the essence of your being that the Creator God has permitted every image perceived, every aspect of every action, and every stumbling block encountered along the way. Gratitude held in the forefront of the mind and heart ...within your very core ...must underlie the focus of your life if there is any possibility of your rising above the mundane realm of happenstance into the arena of true self-determination.

One must be willing to relinquish all ties to the inclination of placing blame external to oneself, and to taking the credit for results achieved. For both ends of that spectrum are rooted in the Divine Will of the Creator. And it is only by His permission that all things ...the so-called "positive" and the so-called "negative" expressions of personal will ...are capable of manifesting in the physical. One must be willing to rise above circumstances and realize that, even in the case of adversity, gratitude must be felt and genuinely expressed for that opportunity to expand one's experience and demonstrate one's knowingness. It may at times seem that the results are unjust. However, Divine justice is not based on man-made logic, but on an infinite system of intricate complexity, in which events may counterbalance events happening in the so-called "past" or the so-called "future."

A disproportionate release of positive or negative energy forces requires a corresponding balancing out. And these expressions of energy are the ways in which energy is permitted to manifest and be perceived by the linear monitor of your awareness in the physical. Each event that occurs in your life is a manifestation, then, of the sum total of your intention, your past and future choices relevant to the underlying point of that particular exercise and the 'state of being' you bring to the particular moment.

The energy you project into a potential manifestation or event determines in large part the magnitude of the expression. An outcome that does not please you or measure up to your expectations is not necessarily an indication of your own shortcomings in that particular moment. But may be a karmically determined outcome that is necessary to counterbalance an activity occurring simultaneously in another reality ...in what you may believe to be 'another time.' Or simply may reflect your own lack of awareness of the role of Divine Will and your unwillingness to acknowledge the Creator for his role in shaping your reality for the optimum benefit of your developing soul-self.

All things are energy. All thoughts are energy. All events are energy. All ideas are energy. And all take their place in the perfection of the totality of all there is. Know this to the very depths of your being. And consider the implications of your every thought and your every action BEFORE permitting it to manifest in the physical. Monitor your attitude before approaching anything and everything. And monitor your response to events as they occur. For without sincere appreciation to God for EVERYTHING you experience ...for everything you are PERMITTED to experience ...the opportunity to balance the energy completely will be only partially realized. And it will be necessary for you to duplicate the experience ...to repeat the exercise in infinite variations of expression ...until the balance is achieved and, ideally, the lesson is well learned and integrated into the conscious awareness.

The element of Divine gratitude cannot be overemphasized, for it adds the essential 'charge' to the equation necessary for karmic completion of that cycle. Until that lesson is well learned, one is, in essence, destined to repeat the lesson. With this concept in mind, you can see why there is a pattern that seems to emerge in your life experiences. A sense that the same sort of thing happens again and again. Most often it is accompanied by a feeling of helplessness and self-perceived victimization, and the placing of responsibility on sources external to the self ...and the Creator. In order to break through the pattern of this cycle, it is necessary to rise above circumstances as perceived in the physical and see what is really going on. Most are not willing or able to take that giant step in awareness transformation. And it is for this reason that so many feel themselves to be 'stuck' in an endlessly repetitive cycle of events for which there is seemingly no relief. The breakthrough offered to those whose eyes have been opened, albeit if only a crack, is to be able to truly look at the circumstances, see the pattern, and ultimately complete the cycle, and rise above it.

The reality you experience in any given moment is, in actuality, a symbolic representation. The representation would be of the thought form ...the energy charged 'communication' you put out to the universe for manifestation with every word, with every emotion, with every 'daydream,' with every aspect of your mentalized process. It is in this way that the free will with which you are empowered is implemented and permitted to manifest in your physical reality. Your thoughts are tools with which you create for yourself the lessons upon which your soul-self wishes you to focus your energies. And as your mind 'rambles' with seemingly uncontrolled 'stream of consciousness' thought packages, you are, in actuality, drawing up the blueprint for the events which will transpire and provide you with opportunities for learning and growth. It is possible to harness this power and direct it toward working for you toward the ends you CONSCIOUSLY wish to achieve. And many are now engaged in exercises geared toward strengthening those abilities. But do not underestimate the power of your higher consciousness to co-create with you. Unless you are at the stage of total mind mastery, you will unconsciously continue to program your reality with the scenarios needed to drive a crucial point home.

Do not feel that you are 'out of control' in your recognition that this spontaneous creation is permitted to transpire. Learn from the process by observing carefully the thought processes that pass through your conscious awareness, as they occur. And note the time lag between the occurrence of the thought and its manifestation in experiential reality. Observe yourself. Become aware. Note to yourself how often your thought patterns 'run' like a faucet left on. And how often, if unbridled, those thought patterns feed your awareness with perceptions and opinions that carry a negative charge. Observe the manifested result of this activity. And in conscientiously continuing to monitor yourself, you will, before long, become able to filter out nonproductive activity and occurrences by catching yourself in the act of creating them. It is a fascinating process, once one acquires the 'knack.' And it is indeed possible to spare yourself much unnecessary aggravation by HALTING the thought before allowing it full expression. It is a skill to be cultivated by all who seek self-mastery.

Major life lessons, however, will continue to be programmed into your consciousness by your higher mind, so that you are able to complete your life's mission and master the issues on which you agreed to focus prior to coming into this incarnation. Do not become frustrated if you are not able, instantly, to manifest love, wealth, harmony, and total freedom from strife, simply because you recognize the validity of the process and force yourself to "think positive thoughts." Much work is done in dream state. And it is during that time that the essential 'messages' are documented and released unto the universe for manifestation in your reality.

Do not assume that you have 'failed' somehow, if you are not able to create perfection and utopia for yourself. For that is not the purpose of incarnating upon the earth plane. Rather, it is the objective to create for yourself the appropriate trials and challenges that will cultivate real inner substance. As you 'handle' each hurdle, encounter each difficulty, and stumble headlong into each so-called "defeat," you will, in fact, have achieved the highest objective of your soul-self, which is to create testing conditions, tailor-made to your ability to handle adversity.

It would seem obvious, to anyone who takes a moment to think about it, that the world ...and all within it ...is confronting continuous problems and setbacks. It is not necessarily a failure that this is so. For it is in the testing conditions created that individual growth is determined. Unfortunately, for so many, the lessons were not well learned, and the physical plane descended into a spiral of negativity, compounded by negativity, as the necessity for repeat experiences became continuous.

The times ahead represent the efforts of the higher powers to intervene and co-create with you the world as it was intended to be. A spirit-centered world of oneness with all God's creations. Much purging is necessary to achieve that state of physical perfection. Prepare yourself for the inevitability of that purging. And know that by shifting your conscious thought process in every given moment, to the optimum positive charge of the energy you project into the whole, that you contribute to the purification process.

Focusing your thoughts in tandem with the thoughts of others on concepts such as "peace" and "harmony" amongst your fellow humans certainly contributes significantly toward the outcome to be achieved. These efforts serve to 'defuse' the extreme measures that might otherwise be required to effectively achieve those ends. Training yourself to project positive thought forms toward your fellow creatures; manifesting unconditional love toward all things; not demanding that the world live up to your personal expectations; accepting reality as that which IS, yet striving to continue envisioning it as it could be; not pointing a finger at others and placing blame external to yourself; recognizing the part you play, simply by being present, in the creation of the totality ...all these things contribute in a positive way toward what we strive for together.

Operate with compassion and loving-kindness toward everyone and everything. Release that negativity which is unwelcome, simply by walking away. And do not contribute toward its escalation by thoughts of retaliation, in the name of so-called "justice." For justice is not yours to dispense ...but God's. Trust that the perfect countermeasure will be provided, in all cases, for misdeeds enacted upon you. And do not take it upon yourself to create that result. Allow the universe the power to exercise its own perfection. And watch the results. You will be amazed in the difference in your own circumstances, when you allow yourself to let go of negatively charged 'hooks.' It is not necessary to respond in kind. And it takes great discipline to train yourself to refrain from the instinctive inclination to give someone "what he deserves." But the results possible by 'short circuiting' the process are impressive.

Disciplined thought and disciplined emotion are skills to be cultivated by all who consider that their focus is in truly being able to make a difference for the overall well-being of the human race. They are skills that cannot be mastered too soon. There is no time better than right now to begin, and no aspect of your training that is more important, nor more potentially far reaching. For it constitutes the bridge necessary to manifest the proof that "you CAN get there from here." And once you are upon that bridge in earnest ...you are halfway home.

8

THE moment has come, for those who consider themselves to be on the Spiritual Path, to look beyond the constraints of conventional wisdom and reach beyond the barriers set down by centuries of cultural conditioning. Many have difficulty with the conflict they perceive between recently encountered Divine truth and the limitations posed by truth as presented in traditional religious scripture. It must be understood that the information presented to mankind by Divine sources is a direct reflection of the receptivity of the audience. That state of spiritual readiness has served to determine, throughout the ages, the level of Divine truth that a particular group of people was permitted to receive in a given time frame.

Spiritual development is not a static condition, but an ever-evolving one. Strict adherence, in these times, to a perspective presented thousands of years ago, reflecting the state of spiritual development of THAT population, is to deny that spiritual progress has been made by the human race ...and to restrict oneself to that level of limitation. The evolution of the soul of man is a fact. You are not the same being, incarnate in these times, as you were, spiritually, when perhaps you were incarnate in the time of Jesus or Buddha. And just as it could not be considered a sacrilege to experience spiritual growth in the years and lifetimes which have transpired, so it should be considered a reflection of that growth that mankind is now ready for more sophisticated information.

The restrictions imposed by traditional religious organizations, which would have you believe that anything outside of the original scripture, which inspired the growth of that particular religious persuasion, is sacrilege or inspired by dark forces ...are a reflection of fear. Those now in positions of authority within those organizations are often impelled to protect the intricate power structure that has arisen from what was initially a simple expression of spiritual truth. And in so doing, would exercise political control over the hearts of those who recognize in that religious tradition the Divine essence in that initial truth.

God has not limited man in his growth. Yet, man seeks to limit God. Those in positions of power within many religious organizations today would have you believe that you have strayed from the path because your inner knowingness is drawn to the higher expressions of Divine truth that are coming forth now as a reflection of THESE times. It is necessary for you, whose hearts are thus divided, to draw a distinction between the respect and devotion that you rightfully feel for the religious tradition that was your cultural birthright in this incarnation ... and your need for an elevated level of spiritual understanding.

It is entirely possible to embrace both approaches without one negating the other. The key to this spiritual balancing act lies in your recognition that each represents truth ...but from a different perspective. For, just as your soul does not consider it blasphemy that you perhaps embrace Christianity in this lifetime, whereas in a previous incarnation you may have been a devout Hindu or Buddhist ...the very fact that your spiritual hunger has drawn you to metaphysical exploration indicated that this too is an aspect of understanding relevant for your growth.

It is likely that, in the countless incarnations you have experienced in this dimension and many others, to have attained the level of openness to Divine truth indicated by the very fact that you are reading these words, you would most probably have experienced and embraced the full spectrum of religious experience available in the history of this planet. Some of these experiences, in all likelihood, would pre-date recorded history and would reflect a level of spiritual knowingness that parallels, if not exceeds, the level of understanding being made available on a widespread basis in these times.

There were cultures, countless thousands of years ago in your planet's history, when man was, essentially, a spiritual being. He had not yet corrupted his environment nor polluted his soul with the karmic debris of negative emotion and negative action that has brought mankind to the imperiled point at which he finds himself today. In those times, the spirit was pure. It was every individual's birthright to communicate directly with the higher forces of the Light, and to radiate Divine healing energy through and from the physical body.

It was a natural state of being and certainly nothing extraordinary, in those times, to perform feats that today are considered 'supernatural' or 'magical.' Wounds could be healed instantly with a touch of the hand, with a concentrated focus of energy directed through the eyes, or with the breath, to name but a few techniques these elevated souls had at their disposal. Illness was almost unheard of. Suffering was a rare occurrence. Human beings operated out of fairness and love for their fellow beings and for all God's creatures. And peace and harmony reigned over all the earth.

How far we have come from those Divine beginnings. How far we have digressed from the Divine vision of the Creator when he conceived and manifested the physical expression of his love. How we have distorted and fouled his garden. How we have let our egos reign supreme and guide us to lord our achievements over our fellow creatures. How we have sought to elevate our own stature, irrespective of the detriment that may have resulted for others. How we have cheated and broken the UNWRITTEN Divine commandments with which each soul was imbued at conception. How we have triumphed technologically and failed miserably as God's children. How tragic that it has come to the point of no return for the homeland of physical creation. But that is the point at which we now stand. That is the point of no return that must be PASSED ...in order that the human race be permitted to come full circle, and to recreate a true spiritual civilization on this physical plane that reflects the original creation, and the loving intentions with which it was formed by the hand of God.

These times are about completion. These times are about resolution. These times are about remembering ...about recognition of the Light energy that is now pouring onto this planet from the Divine realms. For, at the deepest level, there is something wonderfully familiar about this Divine energy so many are now sensing. And something profoundly peaceful and reassuring in the sense of connecting with a past knowingness so distant it defies imagination ...and yet it is here.

That is the nature of the experience many have tasted fleetingly and some are drawn ...even compelled ...to follow to the ends of the earth. For in so doing, they know, at a level of knowingness they cannot begin to identify, that they have somehow returned from whence they came. That is the journey upon which you have embarked. The journey without end that will lead you back home ...to the beginning. If you choose to go.

9

THE question of whether or not to give credence to one's newfound awareness marks the onset of the condition known as a "crisis in faith." These seeming setbacks are not actually setbacks at all, but major hurdles to be encountered and transcended in order to move on to higher elevation and spiritual growth. Profound doubts as to the validity of firsthand experiences that one had come to embrace and to trust are a viable part of the growth process. For what may appear to be a step backward on the path, in truth heralds an impending giant step within the emerging consciousness.

It is important for you, who will be in a position to guide others coming into their power as spiritually oriented beings, to understand the symptoms and the significance of this phenomenon, so as not to misinterpret these signs. Profound doubts, depression, a sense of loss of orientation, rootlessness, the devoidance of material evidences of security, rifts with close family and former friends, the sense of being in living limbo, waiting for a sign ...

all these are classic signposts on the path of those destined for spiritual transformation in this time frame. These tests of faith are moments of catching one's breath and purging oneself of any lingering self-limiting negativities. It is an opportunity to present the current state of being to oneself for review and reaffirmation, to insure that one is still on track. It is an intensely personal process, and must, if full benefit is to be attained, be experienced and processed within one's own depths.

Those seeking easy answers, or consoling words from external sources, will only lengthen the time required for the completion of the process. For the objective here, for those destined to function at the highest levels, is the total relinquishing of all ties to the physical. For many, this weaning process is difficult and painful ...for others as easy and natural as breathing. Within the elevated state of being, there is no place for the concept of 'need' of anyone or anything. The transcendent being is self-sufficient in all aspects, and finds no lack within that could be satisfied by the addition of another individual or an external situation. This individual recognizes the perfection of the situation in which he finds himself. And knows without question...and with a profound sense of gratitude ...that the situation is what it is for reasons that have to do with his own highest good, even though those reasons may not be consciously available in the given moment.

Tests of physical hardship may be permitted the emerging individual as a way of schooling him in particular aspects and giving him crucial lessons on which he is working for mastery. The very issue that the individual may struggle with is, in all likelihood, that which he is destined to transcend completely and teach others by example. The strength must come from within, not from external sources of comfort or companionship. Answers to profound questions come only from within when they represent transformational breakthrough. External answers limit one to the intellectualization of concepts for which there is not sufficient spiritual foundation on which to build.

For wisdom is not permitted until the correct conditions are present within the emerging individual. And a painstaking weeding-out process is a necessary and natural part of the exercise.

It is not at all unusual for an emerging Light worker to suddenly relinquish all ties to family and friends, or to undergo a career crisis of major proportions, possibly leaving one's former profession entirely in preference to a series of seemingly unfocused activities that seem based in short term sustenance without the scope of future growth. The individual appears unconcerned with matters of financial security, as the sense is ingrained deep within that such security is perhaps no more than an illusion and as such is worth little, if anything. There are no guarantees in the coming time frame ...no life insurance, to be sure. No insurances of any kind. One learns to live on the wind, going with the impulse of the given moment, growing from the lessons presented in the order presented, and knowing that the situation is utterly perfect as it is, without requiring reasons to justify mentalized doubts. There are no doubts. There is a sense of total trust in the knowingness of one's highest self that the path is one's true path, and that each bramble encountered along the way has been placed there strategically for reasons of long-term growth and benefit, which are most likely not apparent in the moment.

It is quite common for individuals undergoing profound spiritual transformation to experience bouts of severe depression and a profound sense of loss, which may be focused or unfocused. It is as though the individual were in mourning ...as though someone or something had died. And this sensing is perhaps the most appropriate description of what is, indeed, transpiring within. The death, by disassociation, of the old focus of a consciousness that defines the self as an extension of various aspects of the physical ...is often graphically documented by the systematic 'loss' of all ties. The process is not, in fact, a loss at all, but a relinquishing of the limitation of ties to anything whatsoever. That ultimate state of self-sufficiency is the goal toward which each now on the path is striving at one level or another.

The process is not one that is achievable overnight. For some it is a gradual process that may not proceed a great distance. For others it appears sudden, drastic ...as if one were witnessing the total annihilation of an aspect of one's being. Each is on his own time schedule in which certain objectives must be achieved in order to move on. When there have been significant setbacks in what might have been a gradual process, that individual is faced with the dramatic acceleration of events that make it appear as though all events were happening simultaneously. This drastic a situation is necessary where the level to be attained is sufficiently high and the time frame in which to achieve such growth is limited. The individual caught in the whirlwind of such radical transformation may, at times, question his own sanity. But the knowingness from deep within serves to assuage the violent upheavals somewhat and turn the individual's focus to that place within where all answers lie.

It is wise, during the time of these trials, that the individual focus his energy on one particular aspect of his mundane sustenance effort. And cease to torture himself over the apparent devoidance of far-reaching perspective. This overview comes with time, after the storms have calmed and the clouds have cleared. Generous periods of quiet time spent in contemplation, preferably while communing with nature, are beneficial in helping one to process the spiritual issues at hand. Lengthy attempts to interact with others and have external guidance intervene are counter-productive to the objective of this exercise. Addiction to the attendance of workshops where lost sheep commiserate enmasse is a recipe for limitation. For the very growth the class purports to foster is stifled by the transference of responsibility from the experiential source within the person in the process of transformation ...to the externalization of the experience by looking to another person's so-called wisdom to provide understanding.

For the individual who is seriously seeking enlightenment and has volunteered to serve the Light in the capacity that best matches his abilities, the opportunity afforded by a proper crisis in faith is unmatched in its potential for radical empowerment and facilitating the taking of giant leaps in consciousness. The test is not easy, nor is it painless. But neither is the path that lies before those who have chosen this role in this lifetime. Understand that the seemingly 'negative' occurrences that suddenly appear to befall so many candidates for spiritual elevation are, in truth, no more than an exercise in strengthening the spiritual musculature needed to carry on in the coming times.

What is being tested now is the ability to withstand the winds of change on many levels, without the crutch of the familiar on which to fall back. One's resourcefulness is being tested. One's inner foundation is being strengthened. And the limitation of one's attachment to any and all things external to "Source" is being irreversibly severed. In so doing, one will discover he is no longer tethered to those things which he formerly believed provided the safety of earthbound self-definition ...but, unencumbered, is free to fly to the heights of human experience and ride the winds of change.

10

WHEN it becomes necessary to abandon the previously accepted focus of one's life, it becomes clear as to the seriousness of
the times now upon us ...and the validity of the impetus driving
you toward transformation of your life's perspective. Until the
necessity for drastic alteration of the course of one's life is perceived, one can continue to intellectualize "the calling," and
relegate it to secondary status amongst the list of obligations
that continue to vie for one's time and attention. "The calling"
requires a radical turnabout in the tendency of so many to fragment
their energies and efforts. And presents an opportunity to perfect
the skill of undivided focus.

You who have volunteered to serve the Light in these times
have been taken, in many instances, at your word, as one by one
the realization of the sacrifices that would be necessary become
apparent. One finds oneself compelled, often quite suddenly, to
terminate long-standing relationships which, if left to continue,
would have become an energy drain and a detriment to the

focus of your efforts. It is to be expected that the other parties involved in these 'breakups' do not understand the impetus behind such actions, which come, seemingly, 'out of the blue.' Most often, the Light worker himself does not fully understand why he experiences the undeniable urgency to sever all constraints, and develops an aversion to the very concept of such constraints. Real understanding of the dynamics of this action does not become apparent until one is able to see the common thread of completion and release interwoven amongst all aspects of one's life. For inner transformation does not limit its effects to the internal process of evolvement, but manifests in the outward expressions of all one is becoming.

Do not despair at the prospect of witnessing the structurization, which represented who you believed yourself to be, dematerialize in the wake of the momentum driving you to become something more. That is a necessary ingredient in the process. And though the experience of this severing of ties may be painful to all involved, it is essential to the mission before us now that you are able to serve unencumbered.

Approach with dignity and with compassion the task of becoming wholly unto yourself, in every aspect, and be not burdened by the fear that you alone are experiencing the effects of your commitment to serve in these times. For the nature of the process is universal. And though the timing may differ from individual to individual, and the circumstances may vary, the end result is consistent. For, in emerging from this painstaking process, you will have learned to 'source' inner reserves of strength and understanding that might have eluded you, had you permitted yourself to continue to be dependent upon an external 'support system.' And though you may feel deeply the sense of separation from those activities and those people who provided a comfortable sense of the familiar and the 'known,' you will soon emerge from that period of 'mourning' with renewed vigor and with a sense of inner-directedness that will give new definition to your image of 'who' you are.

There will be difficulties, moments of depression, and feelings of loss of inner direction. But this is all part of the process of clearing out. Once realignment is established with the higher Divine purpose for which you volunteered your time and efforts before coming into this lifetime, the way will become clear. And the path will emerge, unobscured by the limitations imposed by linear, material plane vision.

Your primary obligation in these times is to the ultimate development of self. And though you will coexist and interact cooperatively with others whose life destinies are thus directed, nevertheless, upon this path you MUST stand alone. For, in the end, you are answerable only to yourself and to the Creator for all that will have transpired. Learn to source your inner reserves of strength and your unquestioning knowingness of the love of the Creator, in the times that may prove difficult. For in this connection is your bond of trust. One not oriented toward a reliance upon others based on any self-perceived 'need,' but based on a self-acknowledged connectedness to the God-source within, and from THAT orientation, a ONENESS with all Creation. It is from that position of total SELF-reliance that your potential for Divine service holds the greatest potential for full expression. And in that bond of trust with the Creator, lies the key to true self-realization.

It is for you who strive toward mastery in this lifetime, to establish within yourself a willingness to begin that process now … to acknowledge within yourself that it is not an easy task, that the going may prove very rough, and that you ARE willing to follow that direction unconditionally. Once you have made that agreement with yourself, the concept of 'compromise' for the sake of what others may think, want, need, or try to demand of you, can be recognized as detrimental to your own direction. And your resolve not to be deterred from your commitment to the best interests of your own growth, and your potential to serve to the fullness of your capabilities, can be strengthened.

Often, having to say "no" to someone else is the most difficult portion of this training. For all ploys can, and in all likelihood will, be employed to sway you from your resolve. Your ability to remain steadfast under these conditions will determine the extent to which it will be necessary to repeat this exercise, until the lesson is learned to the extent that it becomes an integral part of your being. Every action you take is a step upon the path. It will either be a step forward or a step backward. And your choices alone make that determination.

If the activity proposed by another is perceived as not being one that will enhance your own higher purpose, you must confront the situation from the standpoint of obligation to self. And as difficult and unpleasant as it may come to be for others to come to terms with your choices, you must stand firm in face of that adversity, and prepare yourself to accept the full consequences of YOUR choice. The concept of adopting a 'compromise position' is counter productive to the objective of such an exercise. For the objective is not in 'keeping the peace,' but in paving the way for progress ...YOURS. By keeping that focus, by refusing to allow anyone or anything to divert your attention from the direction in which you have chosen to travel, you minimize the length of time and the amount of effort you will be required to expend to reach YOUR destination.

This is a path that can only be walked singularly. You cannot hope to make the complete journey by attempting to carry others on your back. And if those others are fellow travelers who also consider themselves to be upon the Spiritual Path, it is crucial that you force them to find the inner resources to walk alone, by refusing to become a spiritual crutch for anyone. There is just so much help that you can provide for another. There comes a point where to be seemingly 'cruel' is the greatest kindness. And though they may not recognize the lesson for them at the outset, though they may accuse YOU of self-serving motives and of ego for your refusal to bend to their wishes, nevertheless, in time, it is hoped that in the firmness you demonstrate, they will eventually recognize the strength that could be their own. Once the lesson is fully integrated, the student becomes the teacher. And he, in turn, will be provided with opportunities to facilitate that growth process for yet another who may be 'limping' down the spiritual path, waiting for someone with the courage to take away their 'crutches.' Whether you are presently in the position of teacher or student is no matter. We all play both roles in this process many times, interchangeably. In much the same way as teachers in mundane aspects of material plane knowledge take a 'refresher course' now and then. Do not assume that you have necessarily had a spiritual setback because you suddenly find yourself reenacting an old scenario. It would merely be your own way of insuring that your inner resolve and inner strength remain fortified. You can expect that you will be 'put to the test' time and time again in your journey. And that it is in your very best interests that this be so.

In the present period, it is necessary to look carefully at the external demands being made of you, and weigh honestly the relative merits of the apparent alternatives, in terms of the potential each may provide for your own growth. If the 'needs' of another are perceived by you to be detrimental to your own best interests, it may be necessary to love that person, and yourself, enough to be 'heartless.' For in the final analysis, there is no greater expression of love for another human being ...nor a greater expression of love for the Creator ...than to enable one of God's children to discover the treasure inherent in being true to oneself and to honor it, unconditionally. For once you have tapped into this source, there can be no need to look beyond it ... for all answers. Even the ones to questions you do not yet know to ask.

The Calling

PART II

11

WE will begin this section by stating the obvious. The planet earth is on a collision course with its own destiny. And just as there appears to be no simple means of eliminating the cumulative results of neglect and abuse to this living being of Light, so there is no simple means of altering the prescription for her redemption. It is all well and good that some people have come into awareness of the seriousness of the condition in which the earth finds herself in these times. But even that level of awareness, were it to encompass all of present-day humanity, would not be sufficient to totally reverse the measures which will be necessary to purge her of her condition. For the damage has been done. And even though heroic measures to "clean up the environment" will alleviate things somewhat, it will still be necessary to have some measure of Divine intervention. A full spectrum of forces from a multitude of dimensions will have the opportunity to participate in this massive project. For just as the responsibility for the creation of the condition does not rest with those now in physical form alone, so too does the responsibility for the rectification rest in the sum totality.

All existing souls participated in the creation of the current condition of the planet Earth. And it is the karmic responsibility of all, to participate in oneness with all, in the mission at hand. All will be watching. All will add their collective energies to bring about the circumstances that will take the earth plane from the stagnant sewers of present-day existence ...and catapult it into a New Age of Spirit. In this way, ultimate karmic resolution will be possible for all souls. Not merely for the ones who are presently incarnate. Not merely those whose destiny it will be to remain in the physical after most have departed.

It is important that this understanding be firmly implanted in the consciousness of those in a position of leadership. For with this understanding as a foundation, it becomes clear why there is suddenly a disproportionate abundance of discarnate entities in attendance upon the earth plane. These beings have been given the opportunity to resolve their karmic limitations, conflicts, and differences. And in this opportunity for direct participation, will have the opportunity to demonstrate the level of understanding that will determine their placement in the dimensions beyond this crossroads in time and space.

You see, these times are an opportunity for all ...not just for ones currently incarnate. As Earth's history writes its consummate chapter, all the actors who have performed their roles here have been given their moment for a final appearance, and a firsthand confrontation with the result of their individual actions. All will experience, in this time frame, an 'instant replay' of their own participation and will be given the opportunity to come into awareness ...and enlightenment. If karmic conflicts are released by each person, incarnate or not, the possibility for advancement is strong, despite individual circumstances. For the point of the lesson would have been learned.

The opportunity is being presented, in these times, to confront the negativities left behind, left unresolved, left to fester as energy on the physical plane. The opportunity is being presented to rise above the limitation of human emotions. To forgive those whom we feel have dealt with us wrongly. And to forgive ourselves for the wrongdoings that haunt our karmic histories. Incarnate individuals who have encountered the presence of 'spirits' have often given those entities permission, on a higher level, to return and rise above the levels of negativity that marked their departures and marred the energies of the planet. It is for each to face that negation of responsibility, and to assume and embrace in oneness his own contribution to the creation of that instance of negative manifestation.

The opportunity exists for the monumental growth of all concerned. In some instances it can be counterproductive to the overriding objective of this exercise, to attempt to exorcise discarnate presences rather than allowing each karmic drama to enact its final scene. In re-experiencing physical reality, the entities add to the energy equation that measure of positivity or negativity with which they departed the earth. It would be the addition of that negative vibration that contributes toward the manifestation of disease in the physical body of the incarnate individual carrying the attachment. If the awareness of the entity can be elevated to the level that forgiveness is forthcoming and resentments are relinquished and released, the entity is able to move to a higher station as the incarnate individual makes his own transition and departs the physical realm. Each, in that circumstance, leaves behind that measure of elevated energy that will contribute, collectively, to the karmic vibration of the planet. And it is that collective vibration that will determine the severity of the measures required to purge the planet, and 'wipe the slate clean' for the emergence of a new Spiritual Civilization.

It is possible for karmic resolution to take on many forms, and should not necessarily be regarded as negative intrusions.

For the truth lies in the balance, and few things are black or white. A Light worker who discovers the presence of another consciousness within his awareness should not see that as an indication of having fallen from grace. Rather, it is an opportunity to purge oneself of the karmic baggage carried into this lifetime, and an opportunity to further elevate oneself for the time of reckoning. By drawing into one's sphere of existence the greatest possible quantity of Light energy, either through direct exposure of the physical body or through vibratory augmentation through actions of a positive nature, it is possible to elevate the vibration not merely of oneself, but at the same time elevate the vibration of the entity or entities one carries through the final scene of this drama.

Re-analysis and reassignment will be available to all who complete the exercise. The greater the karmic debt one carries, the greater the burden of resolution required and the more difficult the challenge to elevate the levels of all involved. It is, in essence, a race against time now, to determine whether karmic resolution can be achieved in time and to the extent that the physical body is allowed to remain. For as the levels of vibration on the planet are elevated, the physical body undergoes the test of being able to withstand those levels. If the level of vibration of the physical body continues to rise in correlation with the acceleration of the planet as a whole, the chances of being able to sustain physical life are increased. If the vibration of the physical body is diminished as the vibration of the planet increases, the likelihoods are great that the physical body will succumb to disease and will perish.

So, you see, the challenge is great. The trials are profound. And the opportunities are limitless. Miracles are indeed possible here. But it is more a question of collective free will than individual determination. For in this lifetime, one carries to the finish line the sum total of one's karmic history, not just the sum total of the circumstances of the present lifetime. Extraordinary measures will be necessary for many to overcome the depletion that karmic debt contributes to the final analysis. The devotion of one's life to the service of God is a path many will choose, without fully understanding why. Yet, on a soul level, it will be clear that that is the only way to undo a history of negative vibration of which they have no conscious awareness or understanding. It is in total, selfless service to God in the coming days, months, and years that monumental strides can be taken and sufficient spiritual elevation can be achieved to enable the physical body to sustain life.

Most on the earth plane in these times will relinquish their physical bodies to their ignorance of their connection to the God-force. This condition alone would relegate the vibration of the physical body to a level which would be unable to sustain life in the conditions of the coming times. For these individuals would have ignored the signposts along the way that might have raised awareness to the level that acknowledgment of the Creator would have been possible. But, blinded by the realities of the physical and bound by the intellectualization of its limitations, many supposedly 'intelligent' people still argue vehemently that there is no God.

It is in this denial that physical destruction takes root. And in this ego-centered myopia that the focus becomes bound in the physical and the destiny of the soul is relegated to the lower rungs of the evolutionary ladder. Many will perish in the coming times, clinging firmly to these beliefs and feeling that the seeming 'injustice' of certain conditions is a confirmation of that position. Rather, it is in the broader perspective of spiritual evolution that the Divine forces bring upon the human race the ultimate test ...to rise above the physical. To embrace the God-centered knowingness of the heart. And to be at peace in the knowledge that His Will be done, regardless of how it may appear for the opportunity to establish heaven here on earth. At last.

You who are reading these words are ones who have taken up the ultimate challenge. You are the select few who have risen to sufficient awareness that the necessity to relinquish all things physical, is unquestionable. That the path of the Light warrior is undeniable. Know that you have risen to the test of a lifetime ... against all odds. And that God walks beside you now in oneness, as the realms of timelessness join forces in a race against time. Go with grace and with compassion on this blessed path. For in that gentle space lies the domain of God's kingdom that exists not within the limitations of time and space, but infinitely and eternally.

12

THE subject of this discussion is the concept of SELFLESSNESS.
We refer to this term many times in these writings. And it is
appropriate now to delve into this concept in depth so that a
firm grasp of it is attained by all who seek to overcome the
limitations of ego-centeredness. It is a delicate balance one seeks
to achieve, and oftentimes a lifetime is spent by those who do,
ultimately, master and embody this principle.

There is a recognition, in the initial stages of awakening, of a
oneness with all of God's creations. Ultimately, one reaches an
understanding and a knowingness of oneness with the Creator
and all he represents. It is not enough to merely intellectualize
this understanding. But that is a beginning. In recognizing
oneness with others, with the elements of nature ...the trees, the
flowers, the animals, the earth herself ...one relinquishes, bit by
bit, the sense of separateness that most humans today cherish.
The goal here is to rise above differentiation and open oneself
to the awareness that it is the one God-essence which pervades

all you see ...and much that you cannot ...upon the physical plane. At the same time, an awareness grows of a blossoming sense of "self"...an attunement with that unique essence.

At face value, these concepts may appear to be contradictory. But in truth, they are not. By 'centering' one's self; by focussing upon one's awareness in a given moment, and only that moment; by being acutely aware of one's perceptions, one's inner voice, one's sensings ...one strengthens the connection to the God-source by maximizing the unique expression of that connection which you regard as "you." It is difficult to discipline your mind into maintaining focused concentration and self-perception while the complexities of your day-to-day affairs vie for your time and energy. It takes much flexing of the 'muscle' of concentrated focus to maintain oneself in the present moment and to give full and total attention to the matter at hand, while remaining alert and aware of everything else going on around you. But this is the objective that must be achieved. Thus, there must be a keen awareness of SELF at all times. Yet, at the same time, the aspect of self that would relate to ego-centered orientation ...for one's aggrandizement in the eyes of others ...must be transcended.

It is far too tempting for one who is suddenly discovering that they have abilities that ordinary people consider 'magical' and 'miraculous,' to adopt a 'holier-than-thou' attitude ...and project that upon the world. It is only by Divine permission that some have been given the opportunity to come into the awareness of their natural, God-given powers in the present time frame. It may be true that certain meritorious deeds or a certain karmic state-of-being may have predisposed an individual to being permitted to come into awareness. Yet, to take that gift as an indication that you are somehow better, more 'evolved' or 'higher' in any way than another less awakened individual would be an expression of the needs of ego. And it is EGO that poses the greatest limitation to one's development.

Know that you who have discovered the ability to generate energies from your hands, oftentimes with seemingly 'miraculous' results, are no more worthy in God's eyes than anyone else. You have merely been given a privileged glimpse into a Divine truth. And have been given an opportunity to put yourself to the test of rising to the challenge of opening yourself to this form of Divine service without the elevation of ego. Know that the ultimate task before you in these times is in being able to serve God SELF-LESS-LY. Without considerations of reward. Without expectations of scoring 'points' with God. Without thoughts of appearing great in the eyes of others who have not yet awakened into this awareness. This type of service comes from the opening of one's heart to one's fellowmen to help each whose life you touch in finding his own God-centeredness. It comes of knowing that 'healing' energy does not emanate FROM you but directly from the Creator, with His permission that this be so.

The energy itself is but a facilitator in the elevation of the spiritual vibration of the individual with whom it makes contact, in the hopes that awareness is stirred within that individual and that the self-healing process is initiated. No one can 'heal' anyone else. Symptomatic relief of a limited duration is, of course, possible. But without the integration of the understanding of the true nature of 'healing,' the results will, most likely, be short-lived and the condition destined to reappear after a period of time.

Miraculous 'cures' have occurred throughout recorded history, and you, no doubt, are aware of this. But note that along with the physical relief of the symptoms of disease and illness, one can always observe a radical transformation in the character of the individual in question. A miraculous cure, therefore, occurs when the 'miracle' of the 'healing' energy is perceived at a SPIRITUAL level within the individual, heralding a major shift in that person's focus in terms of his own self-perception and the way he relates to the world and to God.

Those who would argue otherwise, and limit their vantage point to the five physical senses and modern medical science, are doomed, once they contract a serious ailment, to running from one doctor or 'healer' to another, seeking an external 'cure' for something that has an internal source. Becoming aware within themselves eludes these individuals, because they have transferred their 'power' to others. They place the burden of 'healing' upon the one doing the physical ministering to their condition ...without recognizing that they are a full-fledged partner in the process of recovery. Self-awareness is disregarded by so many who could achieve miraculous recoveries if they were only willing to open themselves to the reality that it is they who created their condition and it is only they who can truly 'cure' it.

It is not enough for those who are able to generate energies from the hand to provide this Divine Light energy. It is crucial to the effective result one hopes to help that person achieve, that they become aware of the role they themselves have played on present-day physical ...and past karmic ...levels, and to acknowledge to the depths of their beings that the energy that you may provide is DIVINE and comes to them solely by the permission of God. If they receive the Light of God, and experience sudden symptomatic relief, they ARE capable of manifesting a 'miracle cure.' But only through a radical transformation of self that incorporates a shift from self-centeredness to God-centeredness. It is for 'healer' and those seeking 'healing,' alike, to recognize this essential truth. And to embody it in every moment and with every breath.

Selfless service to God means offering oneself ...one's time, thoughts, and energies ...in every waking moment, for the good of the overall Divine Plan. It means availing oneself of the gifts of awareness and empowerment that God provides, and using these tools to empower others to do the same. It means approaching humankind with love and compassion without empathizing with their problems and therefore embodying the negative vibration of those problems. It means rising above focus on the physical to the vantage point of God-centered awareness ...SELF awareness ...DURING the process of energy generation, so that emotional detachment is maintained, while at the same time the heart is open to the extent that the Light energy, which is the manifestation of God's love for all creation, can flow freely.

It is a balance that is intricate and profound. It is a balance that must be mastered if one is to truly serve the Light with meaningful results and inner growth for 'healer' and 'patient' alike. It is a balance that CAN be achieved if one is willing to work at it. A balance that takes one from the realm of the mundane into the realm of Divine understanding and true empowerment. Recognizing this truth is a crucial first step in this agonizing process. For it is only in the delicate balance between self-realization and selfless service, that true enlightenment can be attained and One-ness with God experienced. This Divine state of being is possible for all who wish it and are sincerely willing to undergo the painstaking process of peeling back the layers ...and exposing ...and revealing ...and recognizing ...and rejoicing in that Oneness. Knowing at the same time that it is your very own essence, which is, indeed, Divine.

The opportunity awaits you now. The opportunity to 'lose' everything. Everything the mundane world had you believing was important ...the distinction and self-definition that kept you separate from your fellowmen ...and from God. The opportunity to rise above your doubts, your fears, and your self-limiting perceptions, and risk looking yourself in the eye. For in so doing, you open the door to the very real possibility that, someday, you will recognize your own God-essence looking back. And smiling at your SELF-LESS, self-realized achievement. Look carefully, scrutinizingly, and lovingly into those eyes today. And ask yourself, honestly, who is looking back ...if you dare.

13

Never before in the history of your planet has there been an opportunity such as the one being offered to you now. It is an opportunity to avail yourself of the sum total of the wisdoms gained and insights gleaned throughout countless incarnations. Ones in which you have been laying the groundwork for entry onto the path upon which you now stand. For some the lessons have been easily assimilated. For others the training has, of necessity, been more severe, as countless repetitions of the underlying theme would have been necessary to drive a crucial point home.

There are many of you who read these words who are still enmeshed in the process of that assimilation: caught between two worlds to which you feel an instinctive affinity, and caught in the logistics of having to choose one direction or the other, knowing it is not possible to embody both simultaneously. It is for you that these words are written. For it is your mission, at this juncture in this particular lifetime, to determine within yourself whether adequate preparation for a step of this magnitude has been afforded you. Or whether additional opportunities, in the form of life-lessons, would be necessary for you to reach the state of inner peace that would herald the beginning of your journey at the next level.

Those of you who feel yourselves to be bound in a condition of 'stuckness' to routines and relationships for which there is seemingly no resolution must begin to scrutinize those situations and determine whether there is sufficient justification for continuing these patterns ...or whether you are merely permitting yourself to continue going through the motions of a 'habit' that offers little more than the reassurance of the familiar. If the situations in which you perceive yourself to be bound no longer nourish your newly emerging sense of self, it is necessary to acknowledge that realization to yourself before steps can be taken to correct and redirect the focus of your life. If one permits oneself to continue to go through the motions of a situation that is alien to one's newfound focus, merely perceiving the grow-ing discomfort yet not coming to terms with the root-cause of that dis-ease, one may choose, at a level that bypasses conscious mind, to manifest that dis-ease in the physical.

It is understandable that many would question how it is possible for one to make conscientious efforts to maintain an elevated level of vibration ...the natural condition of active participation as a Light worker ...and yet continue to manifest the symptoms of physical illness that would indicate energy imbalance. It becomes apparent that the creation of additional conflict within oneself on issues of one's commitment to a spiritually focused lifestyle versus continuance on a path of mundane existence, adds to, rather than detracts from, energy imbalance. Thus, one could well manifest a serious health condition by virtue of the fact of having been unable to make a total COMMITMENT OF HEART to the path on which your conscious mind would have you believe you stand.

It is in this realm of conflict between conscious mind and heart that the greatest potential health hazards lie for those who are marginally committed to a spiritual life-focus. The tendency to discount the possibility that the conflict of indecision could be a causative factor in a health condition, and jump to the more mundane conclusion that perhaps one is not as spiritually advanced as one would have had oneself believe, would negate the potential of the condition as a learning tool. There is no simple explanation for the existence of adverse health conditions. The causes encompass all realms of physical and non-physical reality. And any given number of these factors may interplay to create a particular condition. The propensity of so many to discount causes other than scientifically verifiable factors has limited the progress that could be made, were minds more open to possibilities that lay outside the realm of microscope and test tube.

The concept of heredity is indeed a possible causative factor in the manifestation of disease. For in the genetic coding of a given physical vehicle, lies the potential for any number of conditions. Whether or not the one who dwells in that physical form manifests a particular condition would be dependent upon choices determined by the free will of that individual. These choices can be made on a conscious level, or determined by one's higher consciousness as a vehicle for learning a particular life-lesson. However, the concept of hereditary predisposition to disease cannot be limited to the physical definition of heredity. For it encompasses the potential contributory factors of 'past-life' predisposition to a given condition, as well as factors that are karmically based.

Each individual carries into this lifetime the potential for manifesting a recurrence of a past-life condition that resulted from conflict created and left unresolved in that lifetime. The emergence of a condition rooted in a 'previous' lifetime can be viewed as an opportunity to complete that issue in this lifetime. For it is likely that the conditions that stimulated the reappearance of past-life illness would be indicative of a recurring life-theme that would surface over a multitude of lifetimes until the pattern is broken by one with the ability to look beyond more obvious explanations and begin to probe for and confront deep-seated causes.

It is in the realization of the existence of such conditions that the greatest potential for breakthroughs of a transformative nature lie. For in recognizing that a given health situation defies logic-based, causative explanation, one opens the door to the possibility that the underlying, long-standing basis for that condition may be revealed and resolved. Looking within oneself for the answers that would evade those of limited, material perspective is the approach of choice for those whose objective it is to rise above surface explanations. When one lets go of the necessity to justify one's actions and one's position on fundamental life issues, there often emerges an instantaneous realization of a pattern that has surfaced as a frequent theme in the present incarnation, and quite possibly as a fundamental theme in other lifetimes.

It is not necessary to engage the services of a specialist to reach these understandings, merely to have the willingness within the depths of one's heart to be permitted to know the truth. Often, understandings of a profound nature are presented when one least expects it. The insights come as flashes ...the proverbial bolt of lightning ...when one is in a relaxed condition and is naturally most receptive to the information one holds within one's own being. If intense concentration is employed, as a way of trying to force understanding, the result will, in all likelihood, not be forthcoming. For the answers one seeks in this situation do not come from the conscious frame of reference, but lie in quite another level of mind, not accessible on demand. Sincere prayer to be permitted to receive understanding on a particular issue often leads to the spontaneous understandings that would, if recognized and addressed, prove most valuable. Keeping a written record of major 'revelations' one receives from within one's own knowingness is a fruitful exercise, as understanding is elusive and may slip into obscurity if one has not made the effort to document the understanding in detail, and refer to it as often as individual situations would indicate relevant. When one receives a major clue to a recurring life-theme, be it related to a health condition or otherwise, the clarity of the moment deludes one into believing that the understanding would be firmly entrenched from that point forth. This is, unfortunately, rarely the case. For the common thread that is momentarily visible is, in itself, but a tool with which one must work repeatedly to truly affect the impact of that particular aspect of one's character upon one's life. Once the theme has been recognized and parallel recurring situations identified, one is able to begin to explore the multitude of levels in which that aspect of one's being surfaces and jeopardizes one's well-being at all levels.

Negatively charged emotions that are withheld and not expressed and thus released will, in time, have insidious effects on one's physical and psychological condition. It is necessary to recognize and to release those deep-seated feelings that could, if suppressed, result in life-threatening health conditions. It is not necessary to express that emotion directly to the person or persons who may be directly involved in a given life drama. It would suffice to acknowledge the truth of the emotion one harbors within oneself, to oneself, either within the privacy of one's internal dialogue or in written form. After making the appropriate declaration, it is then advisable to probe deeply within one's heart to reach the place where unconditional forgiveness may be found.

It may take a substantial amount of time before one can advance from the intellectualization of forgiveness to a condition where it is truly felt and expressed at the heart level. Initially, one would concentrate one's focus on the forgiveness of specific individuals with whom one associates negative emotions or deeds. Then, one would offer forgiveness to any and all others with whom parallel experiences may have been shared in other incarnations. At the next level of this process, one asks to be forgiven for the part one played as a partner in that shared experience, be it consciously remembered or inaccessible to memory. Ultimately, one completes the process by reaching the level of being able to forgive oneself. If this exercise in unconditional forgiveness is completed with absolute, heartfelt sincerity ...not merely words mouthed because one feels one SHOULD forgive or be forgiven ...virtually any adverse condition of body, heart, or mind can be transcended and eliminated. This is the part one is able to play in one's own 'healing.' This is the state of unconditional acceptance and unconditional love to which each on the path aspires. This is part of the process of 'purification' in which you are presently engaged. For it is not enough to 'purify' the physical body, if the life essence within remains contaminated by negativity. It is necessary to confront the realities of one's existence, however painful the truth may be. And to love oneself enough to forgive one's own humanness. For it is in recognizing and acknowledging what may be perceived to be weakness and shortcoming, that those limitations may ultimately be transcended.

It is an ongoing process that one, ideally, repeats often, as reinforcement that the lesson IS well learned. For it is only human to slip back into old patterns of conditioned emotional response. And the objective is to break that conditioning so as not to create additional karma with which one must then deal. The emotional encoding one carries forth from lifetime to lifetime is there, ready to be viewed and confronted, by all with a sincere wish to rise above those timeless patterns. For it is a priceless tool, if examined with care, for rising above the limitations that would bind one to a repetition of negative experiences and adverse health conditions. And to be, truly, the master of one's own destiny.

For those who consider themselves to be practitioners in the 'healing arts,' a scrutinizing look within one's own heart would be the key to all you would achieve in this lifetime. For within that frame of reference lies the answers that would transform abilities producing only marginally beneficial results, to a capacity to serve humanity that is truly limitless. For before anyone can consider that they may be able to assist in the healing of another, one MUST first heal oneself. And recognize that the solutions to many of life's greatest puzzles are already at your disposal, in full view of your heart, waiting for you to find the courage to truly look at it. We encourage all who would serve as Light workers in these times to take that bold step. So that you are able to move forward unencumbered.

The Calling

14

THE energies surrounding the planet Earth have begun what is to be a monumental acceleration. Many have felt and noted the effects of this phenomenon. Yet, most are not aware of the significance nor of the underlying reasons why this extreme purging would be necessary. Many are beginning to experience the effects, even now, as the rate of vibratory frequency escalates at what could be considered alarming rates. It is not uncommon for masses of people to experience the effects of this change in ways which could be considered negative. And this fact must be brought to the conscious attention of those who will be leading in the coming times.

The upsurge in the instance of life-threatening illness and 'incurable' disease will become a normal fact of everyday life as the days and months ahead transpire. Those now in the throes of the finalizing of their lives in this present incarnation are experiencing the result of their physical bodies' inability to acclimate itself to the vibratory conditions present on the planet.

Nothing more. The fact that these effects may manifest in identifiable ways which you may classify as certain physical conditions and ailments does not discount the fact that the true underlying cause of all of it is energy based.

Likewise, the dramatic shifts in temperament, which many have experienced within themselves and noted in others, are, in truth, nothing more than a physical demonstration of energy acclimation in action. If one learns to approach any and all encounters with such negative manifestations with that explanation in the forefront of their awareness, it will be easier to deal with individual situations as they arise and to avoid unnecessary conflict. Overreaction to instances where inappropriate behavior occurs can and should be avoided by all whose enlightened awareness could help them and others to recognize the truth in these situations ...and thus avoid the placing of blame on more mundane causes.

Tolerance and understanding will be key qualities with which one must operate in the coming times ...for the physical effects of the energies will be intense, as will the energies of those affected. Feelings of irritability, depression, despair, unreasonable actions, and the like are to be expected throughout the population and will become the rule rather than the exception. One must assume an air of detached strength when encountering situations where this is the case. As the physical body acclimates to each progressive shift in vibration, the mood pattern will stabilize and the person will ...perhaps temporarily ... experience feelings of normalcy. It is important that one not too readily dismiss associations with other Light workers who are undergoing these momentary bouts of energy shift assimilation, for the phenomenon is truly out of one's control ...and moods and feelings will follow suit accordingly.

The fact that a state of normalcy returns, indicates a positive result in the ongoing acclimation process. Were the physical body not progressively realigning with the shifting energies, serious illness would be the manifested result. When heated tempers subside, it should be obvious to all who become tuned in to the nature of this phenomenon, that a state of equilibrium has been attained, and that the individual in question is still very much in step with the pace of the planet and still very much 'in the running' for maintaining physical form. This cannot be overemphasized. For the temptation will be great to take momentary outbursts and displays of out-of-character emotion at face value, rather than to place the burden of responsibility on the process itself.

Likewise, when experiencing dramatic episodes of out-of-character behavior within oneself, it would be advisable to condition oneself to stop and consider the possible causes of such behavior, before indulging oneself in enacting negative emotions. It should become a regular part of the Light worker's conditioning process to evaluate his own feelings and inclinations before taking action in any and all instances where such action might spark negative reactions in others. By asking yourself: "Why am I feeling this way?" "Is this emotion justified by the circumstances surrounding this situation?" and "Is there possibly no valid explanation for this feeling of negativity?" ...much harm and discord can be avoided, and the effects of the negative energy releases can be minimized.

This understanding ...if taken on a larger, more global scale ... could, in theory, help avoid what is likely to escalate into instances of mass turmoil and upheaval. It is most probably not possible to elevate the consciousness of massive segments of the population such that volatile behavior could be contained. One should expect to see many instances of political upheaval, wars, uprisings, and other instances of mass chaos in the coming times as unenlightened souls find themselves, unknowingly, at the effect of the shifting vibrational energy forces. In all likelihood, it will not be possible, on a global scale, to elevate mass consciousness to the extent that this type of situation could be avoided.

It is for those who have come into awareness to accept that these extreme expressions of negative energy release are all in accordance with Divine Will and part of the Great Divine Plan. For a massive purging has been called for upon this planet for these times ...and this will be accomplished in a multitude of ways ...not merely with ecological occurrences, as had been commonly believed. Mankind will, in essence, annihilate itself in many areas of the globe in the coming times. And the behaviors causing the widescale societal breakdown to come will be a primary way in which that purging is achieved.

The way in which varying segments of the population choose to come to ultimate karmic resolution will be both of individual determination and the result of what has come to be known as collective group karma. It is to be expected that great segments of the population will choose to exit this physical dimension enmasse, as a way of resolving and releasing the result of centuries of negative collective karma in those areas. In so doing, the balance would be achieved in the geographic area in question and for those individuals whose ancestry brought about that condition. Such a sacrifice in human life is a necessity if trans-formation of this planet into a domain of peace, harmony, tranquillity, and Spirit-first orientation is to be achieved in the time frame given.

Do not be inclined to feelings of hopelessness and despair in the wake of such inevitable and monumental crises. For the end result ...the establishment of positivity on the planet ...would have been achieved in the process, and in all likelihood could not have done so, in any other way. Tune in to the feelings that arise within you during these times. And strive at all costs and on all occasions to maintain harmony within your home, your workplace, and within your heart. For this level of balance is a key factor in doing your part to modify the negative effects in your own immediate surroundings.

Much can be accomplished on a individual basis in the coming times. Strive to keep focused on the work at hand and strive to maintain harmony within and in your interactions with others. Avoid confrontations and expressions of inner discord. Practice discernment in your analysis of the behavior of others prior to allowing yourself to react inappropriately to behavior and energy that may not be based on circumstance but on energy assimilation. Learn to distinguish between what is logically the result of considered, thought-directed action and what is not. And moreover, act with compassion and with love toward all your fellow beings and creatures. For in so doing, you will make the greatest possible contribution in the coming times.

The Calling

15

THE interpretations of Divinely inspired teachings have evolved, over time, into many widely accepted and devoutly embraced schools of belief. Each has its own individual focus and specified practices that, if followed in totality, would lead the seeker to a state of personal knowingness of the God-source and a condition of inner peace and harmony. Throughout your history as incarnate beings on the physical plane of existence, you have been provided opportunities to experience, and potentially to master, each of the major schools of Divinely inspired thought. In this, the lifetime of ultimate resolution, many have recognized that there is Divine truth in each avenue of religious expression. And that it matters not so much which road one chooses through which to arrive at a state of oneness with the Creator, but that a path is chosen, embraced, and mastered to the fullness possible.

With that intensive focus must be the recognition that other beings have found equally valid paths to the same destination that differ radically in practice from one's own. It is with an approach toward one's fellow travelers that is devoid of judgment, free from self-righteousness and untainted by the manifestation of ego that one is able to most fully experience the spiritual abundance and take the quantum leaps in awareness and inner growth possible on any of a multitude of spiritual paths.

It is self-defeating to approach spiritual awakening with a 'holier-than-thou' attitude and to condemn others who choose to express their awareness in different terms. There is no one best way to come into full realization of God's love. And the discovery that there is, beyond doubt or question, a particular grain of truth that one has stumbled upon in one's own journey does not prove the unconditional rightness of that direction ...nor provide grounds for declaring all else invalid. Those whose recognition of God's love has been accompanied by attitudes of superiority toward those whose religious beliefs differ have diminished their own potential for spiritual growth and have, in essence, canceled out the positivity in their own recognition of Divine truth.

Many have counseled that one should love one's fellowman, and yet, when it comes to putting that teaching into practice, they instead worship the teacher and condemn their brother for failing to subscribe to that myopic focus. The purpose, throughout the ages, in bringing forth bodies of Divine truth, was to offer the opportunity for those in proximity to that cultural area to broaden their soul-perspective ...and add yet another dimension to the foundation of spiritual knowingness that they have built, brick by brick, over the centuries. Because one considers oneself to be a Christian or a Buddhist in this lifetime does not necessarily mean that one has always reached God-awareness through that route. In fact, it is more than likely that, if one has attained a significant state of awakening through a particular path, one has experienced and mastered other very differing directions of religious expression throughout countless lifetimes. Ultimately, a state of total acceptance of the Divinity of all spiritual paths is an inevitability for those who will advance as souls in this particular physical lifetime.

It is part of the lesson to accept with love and without judgment those who are not capable of coming into awareness in this lifetime. For judgment of any kind has no place on the path toward oneness with the Creator. Most of humanity will not attain that level of elevation in the coming times. And to look upon these beings with smug superiority, for their inability to recognize what seems so very obvious to you, is to forego much of the opportunity afforded by that very awareness. Be loving and accepting of all people ...of all creatures ...of all the physical expressions of the love of the Creator. And recognize that each is, for you, a mirror of some stage in your own individual working-up over the ages. Approach these less enlightened souls with compassion, and seek not to foster your own broader understandings upon them. For they are not capable of embracing such elevated truths. They are not capable, at this juncture, of understanding the implications of the evidence of monumental change that accelerates by the day upon the planet.

One of the major challenges for those amongst the growing legions of Light workers is that your mundane world is peopled by ones who are decidedly threatened by your newfound sense of spiritual direction. It is for you to relinquish all ties to the need to prove or to convince those who are thus blocked from seeing the Light in these times. Allow them to be in the space they themselves have chosen. And know that this is the perfect space for them, in their particular stage of development. Do not allow their doubts and fears to influence your determination to be true to your own inner knowingness. For they would, un-wittingly, dissuade you from your path, for THEIR sense of material-based security.

Do not feel compelled to speak out with metaphysical explanations for the events that are and will be transpiring upon the earth plane. Such understandings would not be comprehensible to those who have not equipped themselves with a firm grounding in such thought. They would find exposure to what you would know to be the truth to be frightening. They would interpret your understandings to be evidence of your own personal instability and would use such information as evidence with which to discredit you and activities in which you may be engaged. Let your Light shine forth through your actions, through your attitudes, through the energy that emanates naturally from you. And thus, by example, you will have provided a meaningful exposure to the truth, as you know it to be, without complicating the issue with the question of their intellectual understanding or lack thereof. Let the Light be the teacher. And know that you are but the vehicle for it.

Be willing to let go of all need to 'save' those who do not wish to be 'saved.' For that is indeed their right and their choice. Know that you are responsible only for yourself ...for your own state of beingness and your own level of spiritual elevation. And that you carry no responsibility whatsoever for the salvation of others who do not seek it or wish it ...regardless of how much stake you may think you have in those individuals. Each comes into knowingness in his own time. And for most, the time is not now. For those of you who know yourselves to be on the spiritual path in earnest, there should be no question, as the energies of planet Earth continue to accelerate, that what you believed to be true is, in fact, indisputable. Those who objected, who debated, and who ridiculed you for your beliefs would by then be feeling the effects of the accelerating reality of the transformation of the physical plane. Many of them would have already chosen to make their transition into the appropriate dimensions beyond the physical. And those left would be struggling with the living limbo between the physical and the beyond ... challenged to the limits of their physical and mental endurance by their own stubborn unwillingness to acknowledge the limitation in the belief system by which they define their life.

Those times will be the most challenging for you who have been designated 'caretakers' for those in the final throes of terminal illness, and will have to watch as loved ones choose to perish rather than embrace the truth of a God-centered reality. Total detachment from any personal stake in the salvation of others destined to leave this plane as unenlightened beings is absolutely essential if you are to continue to function in any meaningful way in the times to come. These words may seem 'heartless' at face value. But on closer scrutiny, the concern would be understood to be more for the potential teacher's welfare than for the remote chance that a grain of truth might be implanted in the arid soil of the resolute mind.

Let be what is to be. Do not feel compelled to try and change it. Merely project love and Light in all you do ...in every waking moment of your existence. And allow the higher forces to operate through your vehicle in radiating Divine energy at every possible opportunity. The potential implanted may well be cultivated and brought to fruition in another dimension where the barriers to integrating higher understandings would be less challenging than on the physical plane. Do what you can to be loving and provide what comfort you can to those who have not permitted you to truly help them. And allow them to fulfill their individual destinies through the death crossing ...knowing that it is indeed God's will that this be so. For the love of the Creator is not reserved for the living, but is provided, without limitation, to all his children, in the way and in the measure appropriate for each. When the potential for learning is exhausted, the need to remain in physical form in a particular lifetime, is considered complete.

Be at peace within yourself that the life mission of a particular loved one or friend is complete ...and that the individual has been permitted to move on to a place where further growth is possible for them. Do not be seduced into emotions of sadness and thoughts of your own personal failure for not being able to 'save' someone else. Do not permit others to cast soil upon your beliefs because you may have attempted to create a 'miracle' and 'failed.' Know that individual destiny is at work. And that the greater good most likely would be achieved in these times by the completion of the particular lifetime in question.

There will be massive exits in the times to come. Illness will become epidemic. 'Accidents' will be rampant. Seismic disturbance and unusual weather conditions will claim a toll in human life. There will be much suffering and much fear. And in the confusion you may choose to shift your energies to a mode of calm, determined action aimed at maintaining your spiritual equilibrium under those conditions.

Know that you who read these words and embrace them as truth will be soon in a position to act as pioneers in a radically new realm of existence here on earth. And be not sad for those who have not been permitted such a choice. See their seemingly premature deaths, their sufferings, for what they truly are ...blessings in disguise. Know they will have been spared agonies that may have been, for them, far more severe, had they been spared the death transition in these times. And know that there is but one thing you CAN do. Love them. Simply love them.

PART III

16

INTERACTING with other dimensions of existence is a practice in which many presently drawn to metaphysical exploration are engaged. For those magnetized to this practice, it is crucial to understand that the calling-in of otherworldly forces must be accompanied by the utmost caution and purity of intention. Naive 'dabbling' with seemingly 'magical' powers can be a blatant invitation to beings from realms of existence that would not be beneficial. If one's motivation in seeking such experiences is to appear elevated in the eyes of others, that motivation would come from the needs of EGO, and could leave one vulnerable to manipulation. Much interference is being experienced, in these times, by those who do not realize the responsibility that goes along with opening oneself to heightened awareness. It is with sincerely-felt, God-centered focus of heart that all such exercises must be approached, taking care to request protection from the forces of the Light before embarking upon any such exploration.

There is a certain fascination that accompanies experiences that reinforce one's theoretical understandings of the transformation process. And with it, an almost irresistible temptation to repeat those experiences without the benefit of the guidance and protection that may have been provided, initially, by one who served to open the door to these realms. Far too many so-called "teachers" abound in these times who are inclined to empower individuals indiscriminately and provide them with recipes for opening themselves to what has been termed "higher consciousness." Under the careful scrutiny of an incarnate teacher who respects the potential inherent in such procedures, great progress can be made. The tendency, however, to empower large numbers of individuals enmasse with tools for opening the doors to interdimensional interaction is fraught with risk.

Approach with reverence any and all opportunities into which you may be drawn for such group empowerment. Take the precautions of asking for guidance and protection within yourself before engaging in any exercise that may result in an experience of expanded consciousness. Do not assume that the requests, if any, for protection and the presence of 'guides,' verbalized by one who may be leading such an exercise, will necessarily suffice. You alone are responsible for your well-being. It is not the responsibility of another, regardless of who he may claim to be, to see that your best interests are addressed. It is entirely up to you. If you choose to engage in such group 'empowerment' experiences, know that the level of information and the level of energy forthcoming reflects the sum-totality of the energy of the group present. If the leader of such an activity is not himself in a highly elevated and purified condition, the energies invoked, while perceivable and possibly 'impressive,' may be very dubious indeed.

Do not assume that just because an individual has acquired techniques for transporting his own consciousness and that of others beyond the bounds of the physical, that the experience is necessarily beneficial. Many are proficient in techniques, calculated to impress the unaware, that require no special level of spiritual mastery to acquire. Be wary in these times. Assess the intention and the level of spiritual orientation of any individual who may profess to be empowered with extraordinary abilities. You know, within your own inner recesses, what feels right ...and what feels wrong. It is termed by some as your "gut feeling." And rightly so. For the clues you should source are there within you, vibrating in the area of your solar plexus, indicating to you whether or not it is advisable for you to engage in a particular activity or to interact with a certain individual. It is advisable for anyone who is inclined to exploration beyond the physical, to tune in to the clues provided by one's own physical body. And to consider seriously honoring those instincts.

There are many bright Lights on the planet in these times. And our words of caution are not to be taken as a blanket dismissal of all who are now serving as teachers. Merely to call your attention to the fact that DISCRETION must be employed. Do not be seduced into willingly leaving your body together with a group of total strangers whose collective vibration may not be capable of transporting you to the heights of which YOU are capable. The current practice of leaving one's body just for the sport of it is not recommended. Taking off on so-called "guided meditations" can be potentially dangerous unless the one guiding the journey is qualified to do so. And few in these times are in that position. Far better to spend one's time in sincere meditative prayer, within the privacy of one's own consciousness. And to behold the visions that are lovingly provided for you personally, by the personal guides and guardians whose assistance you have specifically invoked in each such instance.

Meditation is a power tool in the hands of those who recognize and respect the potential gift of illumination that is possible, if properly practiced. It is a ticket for disaster in the hands of those who engage in it 'for the fun of it.' Know this. And be not tempted to run from workshop to workshop and teacher to teacher, hoping that someone other than your own highest self is best capable of guiding you where you need to go. Those who have become addicted to the practice of metaphysical group voyages have placed a ceiling of limitation on their own spiritual growth by continuing to empower others rather than empowering themselves.

Search not outside of self, but within the self, for the answers that are most fervently sought. Do not permit another, regardless of how 'elevated' he would have you believe he is, to coerce you into believing anything, unless that information FEELS right to you. There is an abundance of individuals in these times who profess to have 'psychic' abilities. They would hold you spell-bound with fantastic-sounding tales of 'past-life' adventures and with well-meaning advice on current life choices that one should be making of one's own volition. Be not so willing to give your power away by giving credence to information merely because it has come via one who claims to have such capabilities. There are many who are marginally empowered in this way. And far too often, they are able only to tap into YOUR own mental recesses, and feed back whatever doubts, fears, and misinformation may currently be harbored there. This is no great feat. Many can do it ...with questionable levels of ability. It is highly unlikely that guidance of significant substance would be forth-coming from such sources, in general.

Even as a source of amusement, the practice of consulting 'psychics' can have adverse results if one is inclined to take to heart fear-instilling suggestions that may be given. Even if you have the good sense to take such information 'with a grain of salt,' the possibility exists that, on a subconscious level, seeds of doubt may be planted within you by such ones, which could then fester within you. This leads to uncertainty and confusion ...and to the inclination to verify the information by cross-referencing it with a visit to a different 'psychic.' After running oneself in circles, hoping to get concurring opinions on matters that no one doing 'crystal-ball'-type prophesy is likely to know, you are left to your own devices ...to wonder. Far better to consult your own heart in all matters, and most certainly in matters of importance. For the life choices you make in these times have far-reaching significance for you who consider yourselves to be Light workers. And such choices should not be made under the influence of anyone, and certainly not under the influence of one whose source of empowerment is dubious. Crucial life choices are to be made by oneself, for oneself if those choices are to achieve their potential for karmic resolution and heightened spiritual awareness in these times. There is only one source under whose influence one would wish to be on this solitary journey. THE One Source.

17

ONCE you have encountered Divine Truth, there is no mistaking it. There is much pseudo-truth being bandied about in these times and much total misinformation which is being presented in the name of Divine Wisdom. There is a profound difference which is easily recognizable when you train yourself to perceive with the heart rather than with the mind. For the mind is but a storage and retrieval center of information, with the capability to run that information through the filter of logic and conditioning. Neither of these skills equips you to judge the validity of information that is based in a reality outside of conventional wisdom. Logic cannot help you determine whether a radical, new concept is rooted in truth or is utter nonsense. And conditioning, which is based in the measurable and provable, offers nothing with which to determine whether or not seemingly radical ideas are profound revelations or expressions of fantasy.

For the most part, you can expect that much of the information being disseminated nowadays is, a best, gross distortion of fact . The determining factor in what you choose to embrace as truth and what you choose to discard as rubbish is that sense of inner knowingness that lies not between your ears ...but between your ribs. When in doubt as to the validity of a source of information, tune in carefully to what has come to be termed your "gut feeling." You know all you need to know about what you may hear. The secret is in learning how to listen.

Whether or not you choose to follow certain teachings you may encounter that are classified as pertaining to the 'New Age' is certainly a matter of free will. But know that the phenomenon of 'channeling' enjoys equal popularity outside the physical realm as within it, as high-level entertainment. There are those, currently discarnate, who have discovered the knack of speaking or writing through the physical vehicle of an incarnate human being. Unsuspecting, newly-awakening individuals are easy targets for such pranksters. And unfortunately, it has come to be considered by many people as an indication of advanced spiritual development to demonstrate interdimensional or extraterrestrial contact in this way.

The situation would be virtually identical from the other side ...and is oftentimes an activity that is motivated through the energy of EGO. It is very flattering, indeed, to delude oneself into believing that one is somehow special, 'chosen,' if you will, to be the recipient of what is often disguised as high-level wisdom. It is equally flattering to the ego of the entity in question to see that incarnate individuals respond with awe and wonderment at whatever they happen to say. And around and around it goes, with egos escalating on both sides, onlookers drawn into the unfolding drama, and abundant time being wasted that could be spent in quiet introspection and in Divine service to humanity.

While it is true that the source of some of the misinformation you encounter on a daily basis stems from ill-intentioned sources who use this activity as a diversionary tactic to keep you off track and off guard, most of the so-called 'channeled' information is little more than a seemingly harmless prank ...at least to the prankster. To the recipient of the distorted information, the result can be far more serious, for it opens one to the possibility of receiving such information oneself.

When one is carrying the attitude that not 'hearing voices' is somehow an indication of diminished spirituality, the door is open to manipulation. In general, it is highly inadvisable to offer oneself up as a verbal or written conduit of information for someone who happens to be out-of-a-body in these times. For to open oneself to the seemingly 'harmless' is also to open oneself up to ANYTHING. And that would include entities who would relish the opportunity to create a forum for their views.

Initially, the information may be verifiable, even quite beautiful. But it is doubtful, in all but the rarest instances, that the information remains consistent. Any gap you sense in the information ...any discrepancies or contradictions, any tinge of negativity, any off-color humor or suggestions, any alteration of personality, demeanor, or accent of the entity ...should be a blatant indication of foul play. And your signal that you have been duped.

Powers of discernment must be developed by all who seek or are open to the attaining of higher wisdom. The ability to distinguish between a high-level teaching guide and a 'cosmic clown' lies in one's skill in perceiving energy. For each entity and each piece of information transmitted carries with it a vibration that is identifiable, if one learns to refine these skills. A high-level courier of Divine information will, without exception, carry a vibration of a magnitude that the affiliation is unquestionable. If you are able to feel and sense energies, this would be the time to focus on that skill and tune in to the clues it has to offer.

Oftentimes, vibration is translatable into color patterns that are visible when the eyes are closed. When in doubt, close your eyes ...and you very likely will be able to 'see' the level of entity with whom you are interacting. Colors and color combination patterns representative of the high end of the color spectrum are indicative of a Divine presence. Colors representative of the lower end of the color spectrum, particularly the color red, are to be considered highly suspect. In this way you can train yourself not only to distinguish amongst levels of discarnate entities, but also to establish an identification code ...a fingerprint system, if you will ...to insure that your trust is not being unfairly exploited.

Listen also, closely and carefully, to the information itself. Does it FEEL like Divine Wisdom? Does the information spark within you a note of deep inner recognition? Or does it, perhaps, produce a pang in the pit of your stomach ...or between the ribs. If the answer is the latter, tune out immediately! Your time is much too precious to be wasted trying to decipher worthless data and evaluate questionable personal advice.

Any entity who refuses to identify himself should be regarded as highly dubious. Anyone worth listening to should have no reluctance to tell you openly who he is and his purpose in coming here to communicate with you. Any entity that purports to be 'above' those basics, on which real trust is based, almost assuredly is not worth listening to. Generally, high-level teaching entities do not engage in predicting the future or dispensing personal advice on mundane issues. Any entity whose focus is in that direction should be regarded as an almost guaranteed phony. The chances are equally likely that the so-called 'channel' himself has stumbled onto a way to financially exploit the gullible public and offers nothing more than traditional fortune-tellers. Extreme caution is advised in giving credence to anything that comes from such sources.

Naturally, you are free to believe what you choose to believe. That is your right. But know that in times when spiritual awakening is marked by a thirst for truth, not merely by a magnetism toward the otherworldly and the unexplained, Divine truth is a rare gem in a field of glitter. You can judge its merit by asking yourself whether this is timeless wisdom that will endure or a flight of fancy designed to live ...and die ...in the moment. It is not a question others can answer for you ... although many are willing to try. It is the type of question one can only truly answer for oneself. The type of question you should be asking. Often.

18

INDISCRIMINATE encounters with entities who are not of the Light is a very real danger and a common sign of these times. Many are aware that there exists, beyond the realm of physical reality, dimensions of existence and consciousness. In dream state, and in the practice of meditation which has become so widespread, many have had contact with interdimensional intelligence, and have developed an awareness of the realms beyond the physical. The error many have made and continue to make is to assume that these encounters are necessarily beneficial. Most often they are not.

The practice of meditation can be quite dangerous if unaccompanied by the correctly expressed requests for protection, as has been discussed elsewhere in this text. For in putting yourself into a meditative state, you relax your conscious barriers and, in addition to permitting access to deeper levels of knowingness within yourself, open the door to interaction with external sources of consciousness. Many react to these experiences by feeling flattered that an entity would choose to make contact, oftentimes never questioning the level of the communication. We cannot overemphasize that, for most, it is not recommended to engage in this practice. For, more likely than not, the source of the communication would be an entity that recognized the opportunity to entertain itself and its friends through its connection with you, and would, if you allow it, establish a bond of dependency through which it could filter all manner of nonsense. Such entities are amused and delighted at the ease with which they seem to be able to make a connection with those presently incarnate, and with the level of gullibility they encounter amongst those who are so blatantly open to this sort of activity. It would be as though virtually anything might be said to one who has recognized his ability to perceive such communication. And far too often, this information is accepted unquestioningly as 'gospel,' simply because it has come from non-physical sources.

It is difficult for one not to be swayed by the otherworldly sensations that often accompany these experiences ...and by the needs of ego to believe oneself to have been 'chosen.' Unless the communication is, verifiably, a high-level teaching guide, who readily identifies himself and states to you the purpose of his communication with you, it is best that you consciously disassociate yourself. This means informing the entity in question that you have no wish to engage in further communication with him, that you have no intention of providing him an audience and a forum for his personal views, and that you hereby request that he cease disturbing the privacy of your personal consciousness. It will, in all likelihood, become necessary to ignore the persistence of the voice which could continue to intrude upon you, and would continue so long as the entity is made to feel welcome. If you are consistent in not responding to a 'voice' that you instinctively feel has no benefit to offer you in terms of information or guidance of significant substance, the entity will, generally, tire of wasting his time with you and move on.

It has become far too commonplace that those who have opened themselves to the reception of high-level energies have also become easy targets for the pranks of entities whose egos are inflated at the prospect of 'reeling you in.' You must be extremely wary in these times of this activity, for it has become rampant. And much precious time is being wasted in filling your mind with a barrage of useless detail and blatant misinformation. It is little wonder, with all the distortion of fact that is now circulating in the name of Divinely inspired wisdom, that so many Light workers are thoroughly confused, and do not know who to believe ...or what to think.

It is crucial, for anyone who believes he has made a 'cosmic' connection, to learn to distinguish between that 'voice' and one's own thoughts. Even for one who is an experienced, established, conscious channel, THAT distinction is crucial ...and potentially, the most difficult aspect of maintaining one's skill to the extent that it is consistently reliable and unable to be tampered with. It is vital, in these times, to be certain that one's thoughts and views are one's own and not being planted in one's consciousness externally. The inner knowingness to which we refer so often in this work, is not one that comes in sentence form. It is not a 'voice' within your mind. And it is not perceivable as being external to yourself. Inner knowingness is a silent realization that comes from the depths of your own being in times of introspection.

Often, during the process of meditation, if one has learned to practice this discipline correctly with the appropriate protections well in force, it is possible to open the door to one's own higher mind and, in so doing, access within oneself the answers to one's most pressing questions regarding crucial life issues. To be able to avail oneself fully of the benefits of connecting with one's inner knowingness, it is essential that one train oneself to recognize the signs of interference from other sources, and to take decisive action toward eliminating this disturbance. Do not allow yourself to become swayed by the ego-appeal of being able to claim yourself to be a 'channel' in these times. For, in truth, this is not a great talent, but a phenomenon which is and will become increasingly commonplace, in the coming years. It is NOT an activity in which all are meant to be engaged. And the well-meaning, popular books which have emerged and have empowered the masses to 'dabble' in this way have done more harm in their well-intentioned instructions than good.

It is DANGEROUS, in general, to open yourself up in this way and allow the energy of another entity to enter your energy field. You would not provide a perfect stranger with an open door to your home and free reign within it. And yet so many of you would not hesitate, given the opportunity, to hand a 'perfect stranger' the keys to your consciousness and permit him to barge in on you anytime he chooses. Know that the sanctity of your consciousness is precious ...and private. And that it is a violation of your rights for any entity to enter and take over, regardless of who he says he is.

In instances of communication at the highest levels, elaborate systems have been established, in which the entity and the 'channel' are in full agreement on the nature of their association, the intended purpose of the communication, and the intended use to which the information would be put. Extensive cross-referencing of credentials takes place, both ways. And methods are established through which the channel is able to verify the identity of the speaker before engaging in the communication. Any entity that fails to submit to these basic preliminaries ...or, indeed, fails to suggest them ...is to be considered a highly dubious connection, and one which you most definitely can and should live without.

It is vitally important that those who have thrown open the doors, however unwittingly, reclaim command of their own consciousness now, before deeper inroads can be made. Reinforce your resolve, by training your concentration during meditation, if you are engaged in this practice, and focusing totally on the silence within. For in rediscovering that centeredness and empowering IT, you strengthen the connection within and serve to disengage any hold upon you from ill-intentioned external sources.

There is much backtracking to be done by those who have opened themselves in this way. Reclaim your power now. And cease activities which are likely to lead you into dubious areas which you are ill-equipped to handle. For otherwise, it is possible for your mind to become a scramble of mixed energies and mixed messages that you will be unable to decipher. And that you will have placed yourself in serious jeopardy when you face that 'moment of truth' that looms on the horizon for each of you and the much-needed Divine guidance from within is nowhere to be found.

This is the aspect that should and must be developed and strengthened now. For reliance upon and deference to any source external to your own highest knowingness is self-limitation at best. Know that you already have all the answers you need, readily accessible, if only you learn to LISTEN ...in silence.

The Calling

19

To the casual observer, it would appear that the sum total of the world's political situation represents a monumental acceleration of events, crammed into an improbably short space of time. This would, in fact, be the case. It was vital that the constraints of political and religious repression be lifted in crucial areas of the globe so that individuals in that area could begin to taste and to exercise a measure of free expression that will be instrumental to their participation in the spiritual transitions soon to come. It was essential that freedom of thought and movement be guaranteed if groups of key individuals were to be able to function in their true roles as Light forces in the coming times. It was essential that they be able to speak out and to identify each other in order to establish the connections that will provide the possibility of elevated group consciousness in those areas of the globe.

In these locations, spiritual awareness is still not a subject that is widely talked about. It has not been popularized there in the way that awakening spirituality has been in other areas. These individuals have not had the access to mountains of well-meaning books of advice, to workshops, to public 'channelings,' and to many of the other phenomena that have facilitated the awakening of awareness in other more liberated locations. And yet, the transformations and the inner callings have not been absent in these places. Merely not publicly spoken about. For the individuals experiencing these times under oppressed conditions, the awakening process has been a totally personal, internal one. And in many cases, the results have been more intense and more profound than in areas where there has perhaps been too much talk and too little personal introspection.

Enlightenment is an intensely personal process. And even though individuals coming into awareness under the constraints of oppressive political regimes may have been deprived of the reassurance of camaraderie during the process, they were able to turn more readily to the internal 'Source' for the answers that were not forthcoming elsewhere. Do not assume that, just because spiritual awareness has been enjoyed as a popular craze in the area of the globe in which you find yourself, you are any further along than those in other areas who were forced, by default, to obtain their answers from within.

There are individuals in every area of the globe who today know they have been 'tapped' as informational links with realms of existence they perhaps do not fully comprehend, and yet they recognize the truth that filters through their consciousness ...and have agreed to serve the Light in the present times and in times to come by relaying that truth.

The phenomenon known as 'channeling' has been experienced, and is being actively practiced in every conceivable corner of the globe. Many such connections are of an inconsequential nature, and the recipient of such communication relates it more out of a sense of amusement and entertainment than any other purpose. This activity will wane of its own accord, as people will become quickly bored with an activity that is already becoming commonplace, and the information being relayed is recognized as neither profound nor interesting.

Yet, at the same time, there are those who HAVE made a connection with higher realms of Divine energy, through which vital instructions are being transmitted now, and will be increasingly so in future times. These individuals know who they are. And most have not exposed themselves to public scrutiny, at the request and insistence of the guides with whom they work. These connections are being cultivated carefully, and each team of channel and guide work together to perfect the skills of each in the transmission and receiving of Divinely inspired information. These contact points will play a vital role in the carrying out of instructions for select groups of beings in the times soon to come. It is not the wish of the Forces of the Light to leave crucial matters solely to chance. The element of free will is, in some instances, being supplemented by Divine guidance to insure that the Great Divine Plan is carried to fruition by those entrusted with that mission who have volunteered to serve, in physical form, in these times.

Those individuals who are functioning as 'receivers' now ... many clandestinely ...will emerge, of necessity, as the forces which will magnetize those destined to seed the world of tomorrow into viable communities of ethnically diverse, yet spiritually similar, individuals. Those who have opened their hearts and minds to these words have already identified themselves to themselves ...and to God. They secretly, or more openly, have come to the same conclusions as their brothers and sisters in the far reaches of the globe. And they are united in their ability to expect the unexpected and to deal SELF-LESS-LY with their fellowmen, under ANY conditions.

Many have begun to look around them to quietly identify their 'teammates.' And the recognition crosses all barriers of race, religion, and differences in cultural background.

Somehow, they 'know' a brother or sister on sight. And, most likely, the recognition is mutual. A cohesive force will emerge of those with the courage to act upon the guidance provided and with the willingness to bond together as a 'family' of spiritually like-minded individuals.

The seeds of those families have been planted in the minds of those who are to play leadership roles in the times soon to come. And those seeds will take root, as the days soon to come begin to be counted. There will emerge a sense of urgency to take action ...to DO something ...together. And recognition at a soul level will begin to flower in the eyes and bear fruit in the hearts of those who have heard the voice of truth and have seen the handwriting on the wall. And hands will be joined, without fear of the unknown. For they will know that they are being led ...by the hand of God.

20

WHEN the time comes to translate the sum total of your preparation and training into action, there will no longer be a grace period within which to deliberate the extent of your commitment to the service of God and the Great Divine Plan. There will no longer be the leeway that you perceive, in which to try to have your cake and eat it too ...to be dedicated, mentally, to Divine Service, yet remain tethered to the constraints of the material realm. Those times are soon upon us. And these times are about total focus upon preparation.

As the energies begin to reach significantly higher elevations, you will experience within yourself massive changes, both on the physical and mental levels. What you may not sense directly, are the profound alterations taking place within your spiritual body, even in these times, so that you are equipped to sustain those levels and function simultaneously in this dimension and in the one to which these times constitute a bridge. There is an otherworldliness to the sensations that often accompany these changes. And feelings of differentness and separation from all that had once been familiar are commonplace.

These transitions are difficult to withstand alone, without the support system of others simultaneously undergoing similar changes. The recent emergence of many spiritual organizations has served to provide that this measure of security, support, and reinforcement was firmly in place, so that Light workers in the throes of radical transformation might, at least in part, understand what was transpiring. For those who are fortunate enough to have encountered a spiritually focused way of life, the radical changes so many are experiencing come as less of a shock than for those who have come into awareness singularly. And yet, for those whose destiny it is to make the journey alone, the realizations may well be that much more profound by virtue of the fact that there really IS no one who 'understands.' It is these ones who are most likely to turn inwards for the emotional and psychological support that would not be forthcoming from the outside world. And in so doing they would have encountered the inner resources upon which real strength is built. For these ones would not have the built-in luxury of verification from external sources. And would have been forced to look within for answers that much sooner.

It is difficult to say which situation would be the more fortunate. And that, in truth, does not matter. What IS important is that the reality of the situation is recognized and internalized. That one comes to terms with the truth of what is, indeed, transpiring and to know that this condition is the highest possible expression of who one really is, and all one may well become.

These times are about making peace with it, within yourself. And providing, where appropriate, the loving support that comes from your own inner knowingness, to those who may yet be struggling with the ramifications of all that is transpiring. These times are the rudimentary tests of your fiber in preparation for the times ahead, practice runs in miniature that point out to you your strengths and weaknesses ...tests of courage, of patience, and of endurance.

Choose to see the life lessons that are being provided you, in this time frame, for what they are. Intensify your focus on reaping the full benefit of the lesson inherent in each circumstance you are permitted to experience. And release, once and for all, any tendency to look to causes external to yourself as explanations for why, suddenly, you are enmeshed and inundated in hardships and unrelenting confusion. These situations are only testing conditions, and only a small sampling of what may be yet to come. Those who permit themselves to be swept into a state of panic and despair over the upheavals of these times are less likely to be able to withstand, psychologically and emotionally, the times to come. You must become conditioned now to deal with absolutely any situation with a cool head and with God-centered focus of heart. Know that it is Divine Will that these times represent the culmination of a spiritual cycle, and that the completion of the old is a necessary prerequisite for the rebirth of the new.

As the manifestations of negative release intensify upon the earth plane in the coming months and years, you may be permitted to bear witness to phenomena you would not have thought possible outside of science fiction. But, it will be reality. You may have direct encounters with other life forms, in the physical, whose karmic destiny it is to intervene in these times. Many of these will be representative of the forces of the Light. Many will not.

As this chapter in the history of your planet nears completion, those of more sophisticated perceptions are keenly aware that the planet Earth is in the throes of radical transition, and will conclude that it is 'up for grabs.' Those realms in search of supple-mental territory in which to expand their empires will attempt to claim planet Earth as their own, should chaos reign in earnest and societal breakdown render the unifying systems of your civilization as destroyed and irretrievable. Even in these times, when the realities to come are far from apparent, their awareness has signaled what amounts to a 'stake out' of the faltering territory you know as your world. And they wait, eagerly, for their moment. This information would explain why, in recent years, and increasingly as the Earth's 'moment of truth' draws near, there has been reported and documented, an unprecedented number of extraterrestrial sightings.

The presence of UFO activity in some areas is so intense as to be considered commonplace in these regions of the world. And the publicity that has accompanied this situation in recent years has resulted in a certain measure of public acceptance of the existence of the phenomenon. One is no longer inclined, upon sighting strange light patterns in the night sky, to descend into panic and hysteria. And this is fortunate. For there is little, if anything, that could be done on a widespread scale to alter this situation. Rest assured that your political governments are acutely aware of the presence of 'unidentified' spacecraft. And scientists from every corner of your globe are feverishly engaged in strategies as to how best to deal with what they know to be an escalating situation. Naturally, this government acceptance is not publicly acknowledged, to avoid the mass hysteria which would result. And yet, however unspoken, 'everyone knows.'

What is not known is the proportion of these extraterrestrial presences that are representative of self-serving, power-seeking regimes, waiting to pounce. And the proportion that represent the interests of the Creator and the Divine Plan intended for this planet, who hover patiently and await their moment to come to her defense. This aspect of the drama that will soon begin to unfold is one less often cited in traditional scripture that prophesized the transitions of these times. But nonetheless, it is a viable factor in the karmic resolution issues that will be enacted upon this stage.

There is no cause to be alarmed at this time ...simply cause to be aware. And to exercise caution in actively seeking out encounters with these extraterrestrial presences. In general, it is highly inadvisable to deliberately venture into areas where there has been reported to be repeated UFO activity. It is unlikely that you will find these beings to be the cute, friendly little creatures depicted in recent films. And it is unlikely, in the present time frame, that representatives of either 'side' would welcome your intervention, however well intentioned.

The forces of the Light are well equipped to deal with the situations that may arise in the times to come. It is for you, who have been alerted and given advance warning of the reality of this situation, to discipline yourself toward non-interaction, and to trust that this too is a part of the Divine Plan that must be enacted in order to purge this realm and provide for the possibility that The Great Spiritual Civilization can be established here, as is God's Will.

In time, you may possibly come to witness the clash of mighty armies from dimensions beyond your dreams. You may see with your own eyes life forms that are, in every conceivable respect, 'alien' to your reality. And you may, in time, recognize some amongst them as your brothers, in spirit. For the concept of karmic resolution is not limited to the 'flesh and blood' you now recognize as mankind, but vastly predates that limited expression of humanness. And represents, in its return to this plane, a return to the earth's beginnings and the completion of a "cycle" in every aspect.

Know that all this is as it is intended to be. And do not panic, should you encounter beings that logic would tell you 'do not belong here.' It is entirely possible that they do ...in many respects. Do not be inclined to take matters into your own hands in these situations. Passive avoidance is the approach of choice, for you whose role it is to be the 'ground forces' of the Light. Know that others from every dimension and every expression of Creation have their own roles to play in this epic. And it is no more your right to interfere with this aspect of THEIR destiny, than it is for them to interfere with yours. Know that God's Will WILL be done ...at the appropriate time.

Your task now is to concentrate your focus on the preservation and purification of your physical form so that it will be in service when it is most needed; to begin to apply active forethought to plans for the ongoing lifestyle of your new 'family' ...the brothers and sisters who walk by your side in the Light; and to demonstrate, in your every action, your unceasing gratitude to the Creator for being permitted to serve in this way for the wonders yet to be seen ...and the chance you may live to tell the tale.

21

THE use of crystals and other minerals in conjunction with energy work can be fraught with risk and inherent dangers, if one is not properly schooled in the correct use of these tools. It is proven fact within the realm of your physical science that the mineral kingdom is capable of assisting in energy work, and that its nature is that of an augmentor of electromagnetic vibrational frequencies. What is less known or understood is the spiritual nature of this capability, and the correct procedures for attaining the true benefit of those capabilities and avoiding the dangers inherent in their casual usage.

When working with crystals and other potent energy tools, it is crucial to understand that to do so is to elevate one's vibrational frequency. In the process of so doing, it is not enough to be willing to unconsciously accept whatever comes as a result of it. It is vitally important for those who are drawn to the use of these tools to know that the augmentation of energy vibration is an open door ...an invitation, if you will ...to interaction with other realms of existence.

It was not God's intention to provide his children with matches with which to play. The artificial elevation of ones vibration must only be undertaken with the strictest precautions. Sincere prayer, before beginning to create the intention that the energies be elevated, requesting that protections be provided ...and most importantly, declaring that NOTHING BUT THE LIGHT FORCES OF THE CREATOR GOD ARE WELCOME OR PERMITTED IN THIS SPACE ...is essential. If these measures are not strictly undertaken, it is quite possible that ill-intentioned entities could seize the opportunity to enter the vibrational field created by the minerals employed and contaminate the space which you seek to create.

The intention in providing these wonderful tools is to facilitate in the creation of a holy and sacred atmosphere in which to do Light work. But unless that intention is declared and the crystals themselves are given these instructions, that sacred environment is not automatically forthcoming. Crystals are much like your modern-day computers in that they have capacity and capability, but require programming and detailed instructions with which to equip themselves to carry out your good intentions. They are as dear friends, willingly serving the Light, willingly serving those who have been entrusted with their care. They are powerful assistants, if used properly with reverence and love. They are dangerous ammunitions when placed in irresponsible hands.

Awareness of crystals and their potential 'powers' has been popularized in your area of the world in recent years, and much damage has been done by those who would harness those capabilities in order to enhance their own ego-centered goals. There are many who seek to 'lord it over' others who are wide-eyed with wonder at that which they do not understand. In this way, the one who has access to this power is able to elevate himself in the eyes of those who seek to become followers ...those not realizing that the only power truly worth having comes from within oneself.

The majority of those whose eyes have been opened a crack ... and have recognized the Light ...still seek knowingness and confirmation of that which they sense from external sources. They turn to the teachers and gurus of your so-called "New Age" to provide them with the reassurance that they are indeed on the right track and have not lost their senses entirely in what they increasingly perceive to be true. That reassurance can only be mentalized when forthcoming from external sources. The knowingness deep within one's very core should be the only affirmation needed when one has risen to a level of recognizing the True Spiritual Path ...and realizing that one has both feet firmly implanted upon it, regardless of consequences, regardless of the judgments and criticisms of those who are blinded by conventional human wisdom and a limited, material understanding of the nature of reality.

In seeking to harness the benefit of the bounty offered by the mineral kingdom, one must be willing to truly relinquish all sense of personal, goal-oriented, ego considerations. One must be totally focussed on the concept of doing the work of God. And only this. One must adopt a self less, humble attitude when approaching any energy work, sincerely asking that guidance and understandings be provided ...and only from the highest levels of the kingdom of the Light.

Far too many individuals who were initially drawn to energy work and to the employment of crystals and other minerals in that work, have been misguided by those who awakened into awareness perhaps only months or years earlier. It is much akin to the concept of 'the blind leading the blind.' To place a crystal in the hands of an unsuspecting person, who may or may not be drawn to them, is to place a hand-grenade in his palm with a minute understanding of what might happen when the pin is pulled. To vaguely instruct people to meditate with crystals is potentially the most dangerous common practice of all. For in meditation, unless protection is requested, with a real understanding of what is meant by protection, you have provided that individual with potential danger. It is for this reason that so many well-intentioned individuals who have toyed with crystals have experienced negative phenomena in their lives since they began working with minerals.

The crystals have the capacity to enhance vibration, to open the consciousness during meditative states, and to facilitate the experience of 'leaving one's body,' or so-called out-of-body trips. The naive and curious who engage in this practice oftentimes leave their 'homes,' not having any idea of where it is they are going, and leave the door wide open in their absence. This situation will be as a neon sign to discarnate entities who are not of the Light, to enter and to cause disturbance from that point forth. It is not recommended, in general, to engage in the practice of leaving one's body and roaming about in the realms beyond the physical, just for the thrill of it, or for the sake of being able to brag to one's friends that you have this capacity. This attitude comes solely from ego-centeredness and virtually insures that a good result would not come of the experience. Even for those with the best of intentions and with an open heart, to jump in the deep water ...indeed, in water with a powerful current ...before becoming thoroughly schooled in how to swim, is a dangerous practice at best.

For those who are well schooled in meditation practices, who understand that a request for protection of the physical body is rudimentary practice before engaging in any meditation exercises, and who, moreover, seek to broaden their understanding and gain wisdom SELF-LESS-LY ...that is, in order that they may be permitted to better serve God ...the result may, indeed, be quite beneficial. And it is for those individuals and for them alone, to seek to augment their experience with the use of crystals. For all but those on an extremely sophisticated level of Light work, it is recommended that the entire realm of crystal dabbling be avoided. The risk is too great.

We would advise you not to seek to awaken others by 'turning them on to crystals' unless extreme discretion is used as to who is thus empowered and unless you impress-upon the niave individual that these tools are absolutely, under no circumstances, to be used without instructing the crystal itself to facilitate in protecting the physical body and providing the insurance that no ill will come to it. To instruct anyone to place a crystal under his pillow to facilitate with dream-recall ...is blatant irresponsibility. For in sleep state, one is extremely vulnerable. If this practice is to be engaged in, it is essential that the crystal or mineral be instructed to provide total protection of the physical during sleep state ...this in addition to the programming of any particular understanding with which you wish it to assist.

Those who guide mankind from beyond the physical plane in these times do not wish to sacrifice so many naive and trusting souls to the harsh lesson of the misuse of mineral power. This would explain to you why the once explosive interest in this subject has waned dramatically in recent years. It is with Divine intervention that this is so. People are instinctively wary now of the use of minerals, where once they rushed in blindly, to 'taste' and experience something new and exciting. They themselves do not even know why they are suddenly less interested in dealing with crystals ...only that it somehow no longer attracts them.

It is for the rare ones who have taken the time to study and master the principles underlying all forms of the seeking of enlightenment and higher understanding, to attempt, if you are so inclined, an understanding of the correct use of the gift offered by the mineral kingdom. And those of you reading these words would know who you are. Proceed with the utmost reverence, with caution, and with unceasing GRATITUDE TO THE CREATOR for the gift of wisdom and understanding, in your pursuit of spiritual growth with the aid of the mineral kingdom. For all others ...particularly those who are not prepared to take the time and make the effort necessary in attaining such a thorough grasp of this complex subject ...we would hope you would have the good sense to leave well enough alone and not to play with fire.

Unfortunately, crystals were exploited before their time. It was the intention that these powerful tools be made available to the coming Spiritual Civilization in future times when the wisdom and the understanding of their correct usage would be forthcoming and widespread. Sadly, there were those who sampled the potential inherent in crystals and minerals, and a popular craze resulted that led to their premature harvesting and exploitation. This was not the intention for these times, nor the intention for those now barely considering that they may be seed children for the coming times.

When the age of the Golden Spiritual Civilization is established, crystals will play a major role in facilitating with many facets of 'power' be it intellectual clarification or physical harnessing of electromagnetic energy as a resource in physical terms. When those times are at hand, the crystals will be readily available, for the earth will have heaved and spilt them forth from the depths in which they now wait. They will be there as a Love Offering from the Creator to the children of the new Spiritual Civilization, easily accessible, awaiting the selection of those who have been prepared and empowered to properly use them.

PART IV

The Calling

22

Lɪ𝔱𝔱𝔩𝔢 has been recorded regarding the earliest history of your planet and the cultures that were in existence during that period. Of the information currently available, much is based on speculation and the remainder based on research efforts that are only marginally accurate. It is our intention to fill in those missing pieces. For it is of benefit to most for whom this work is intended, that an understanding of the connection between the more significant of those lifetimes and the present incarnation be established.

The civilization which is today known as Lemuria predates the advent of the civilization known as Atlantis by tens of thousands of years and overlaps only slightly. The two were distinctly different cultures, representing a polarity in orientation. Even though the Lemurian civilization was, in its fundamental essence, more closely aligned to the direction in which your present-day civilization is headed, it was necessary to sacrifice those correctly oriented beginnings in order to allow for the manifestation of the karmic lessons and deeper soul understandings afforded by the lessons of the Atlantean culture. With the assimilation of those understandings, it is now possible to complete the cycle and permit a true Spiritual Civilization to manifest and to flourish upon the earth.

Had the exercise of the misuse of power afforded by the age of Atlantis not been permitted to transpire, it would not have been possible for those destined to seed the coming age of Spirit to do so. It was necessary to permit the full drama to unfold to permit the Atlantean culture to rise to the heights of technological intelligence and to succumb to the temptations of ego: greed, lust and unbridled hunger for power. For through the depths of the drama that was Atlantis, the lesson endures at a level that cannot be forgotten. Each who is to play a significant role in these times carries in his soul memory the poignant aspects of that lesson. And the knowledge that there would be an opportunity to complete the karma created then, someday.

Someday is about to dawn. And with the shifting energies of these times comes a sense of the vaguely familiar. A feeling of somehow having been in this script before. And so it is. Your present-day civilization is no less representative of the gross misuse of power than was Atlantis. The technological differences are significant, to be sure. But the human motivations, whose collective vibration manifested a 'point of no return,' are not at all dissimilar. The times soon to come represent the testing conditions that will determine whether the lessons have, in fact, been learned on a soul level. And whether those who carry the weight of individual karmic responsibility for the decisions which brought about one culture's destruction can apply the understandings gained to facilitate in the present culture's transformation and, as such, its salvation.

The temptation will be great in these ones to defer to technological expertise ...the known, the proven, the verifiable ...to rectify conditions where it is obvious to anyone of intelligence that the survival of the species is in jeopardy. The logical orientation which the present civilization has served to so firmly implant within the conscious mind is the challenge that must be overcome. For the answers now, as then, do not lie in the realm of the rational, but rather in the realm of the spiritual. That which cannot be tested, or proven. That which cannot be seen, but only sensed. That which cannot be touched, except within the deepest recesses of one's heart. That which will determine whom amongst these potential candidates for karmic completion will demonstrate the courage to defy what 'makes sense' for the possibility that the solution lies beyond the logical foundation provided by the wisdom of the times.

This is the test that man manifested once before. Long before he was ready to relinquish his sense of separateness. Long before he was ready to release his need to make his mark upon the illusion that is 'history.' Long before he was ready to truly confront his ultimate fear and realize that there is nothing to be lost by defying the laws of the physical, and much potentially to be gained by taking that risk.

In these times there are those amongst you who will make massive strides toward the accomplishment of that end. There are those who will take the ultimate step of putting their own physical existence on the line as a means of standing up to the testing conditions which will be provided in the initial stages of this effort. For it is theoretically far simpler to advise others to transcend the limitations of the physical, than to do so oneself with a willingness to bear the consequences, regardless of what they may be. Many will manifest such tests of their own tenacity to that which they profess to believe, in order to have personally experienced that challenge. They will have dealt with the resultant triumphs or disasters as apply directly to their own physical survival, well in advance of being given responsibility for the well-being of others.

These ones may assume that such a trial is an indication of unworthiness of higher levels of responsibility. Even in moments of profound despair, one must never lose sight of the understanding that everything that transpires ...all of it ...is but a test. An aspect of your higher training. The severity of a particular challenge is by no means to be taken as an indication of unworthiness to serve, ultimately, at the highest level, but to be recognized as verification of your ability to do so. Through the darkest hours, your ability to retain your higher vision of the true nature of reality, and not succumb to the temptation to defer to consensus wisdom, will determine the level at which you will be permitted to serve in the times to come.

There are opposing factions within the ranks of the spiritually focused, over the issue of whether one places one's allegiance and derives one's justification for incarnation in this time frame from prior Atlantean or Lemurian karmic affiliation. There seems to be, in these times, a polarization of loyalty to one or the other point in history. And there are many who point out with great pride that their karmic roots are Lemurian, and who regard with an air of superiority and disdain fellow Light workers who may have recognized and remembered their Atlantean connections. It is as if these ones were declaring that their own personal history is untainted by the lessons the Atlantean age afforded humanity. That they, therefore, are unburdened by the ego-orientation of the Atlantean times. That they, somehow are spiritually 'pure.' It is obvious to any observer that such an attitude, in itself, constitutes the consummate manifestation of ego. And expressing such a view would be a contradiction of the very point that individual was hoping to make.

Likewise, there are those who cite with pride their Atlantean histories as a means of staking a claim on an elevated station in the coming times, and 'feel sorry for' their more 'primitive' Lemurian brethren. This is no less a manifestation of ego, and the very issue one must weed-out of one's repertoire of responses, if one has any hopes of being permitted to serve at a level of any significance at all.

It could be amusing to witness the present-day factionalizing of one's ancient affiliations, were the situation not in direct contradiction to the entire objective of what is transpiring in these times. How is it possible to declare recognition of one's 'Oneness' with all aspects of the Creation and to differentiate oneself from fellow Light workers who may be suffering from the delusion that they are exclusively 'Atlantean' OR 'Lemurian.' In truth, it is the rare individual who is at the level of recognition of either karmic lineage who does not, in fact, have karmic history in both cultures.

It is important that you realize that there is no inherent 'superiority' to be associated to either of those periods in the history of your planet. But that you recognize that the lessons afforded by each of those times were fundamental to the possibility of karmic completion in these times. Because you may have been given a privileged glimpse of a 'past-life memory' during meditation or in dream state, does not preclude the possibility that you carry an equally rich history in very different times, which has not yet been made available to you.

The point of recognizing such an episode in one's own history would not be as justification for claiming an alliance, as one would to a sports team, but as a vehicle for introspection on the aspects of that incarnation that might relate to current issues of karmic resolution at a soul level. It is for this reason and for this reason alone that those whose life-focus has shifted to a spiritual orientation are permitted to have such glimpses into 'the past.' For to recreate issues of ego, when the object of the exercise is to recognize the role the concept of ego played in a particular drama, is a contradiction of your objective in such an exercise in self-awareness.

Each of the players in the drama that unfolds before us now is equipped with a rich history of incarnations that would have provided understandings and refinements at a soul level ...were the lessons well learned. The extent to which this is so determines the severity of the training these ones are undergoing in the present time frame. The objective in these times is to embrace, with compassion and with love, one's fellow traveler. To set oneself not apart, by virtue of self-aggrandizement or self-effacement, from one's spiritual brothers and sisters. But to recognize that all energy is aligned with the God-centeredness of focus that directs these times. And that each individual who is directed to view himself as part of this effort is no less an expression of that energy than any other. It is this lesson that must be mastered, once and for all, by those who hope to transcend ego. And to recognize, at a level at which one can no longer question, a Oneness with the energy that unites us all.

23

THE true 'history' of your planet, in terms of ancient cultures, has direct relevance to the turn of events which you are encountering in present times. It is through a study of the available information on the cultures of Atlantis and Lemuria that one is able to gain a perspective on the direction in which you, as a culture, are now headed. For those interested in gaining a broad-based foundation in the karmic significance of the present conditions, it is necessary to look beyond the immediate past of verifiably documented 'history' to the very beginnings of culture upon the physical plane, and to ponder and explore the nature of these most ancient cultures.

We are in the throes of the completion of a cycle now and a return to those beginnings ...a re-awakening of the ideals and values with which you, as souls, were created and which lie dormantly within each of you, waiting for the appropriate moment in time for emergence. The simplicity of a God-centered, spirit-centered orientation to life and to living is that which must be re-created in the coming times, if we are to assist in the full execution of the Great Divine Plan. It is toward these ends that we work together now.

Rather than dwell upon the imponderable past, however, and allow yourself to become sidetracked in the intellectualization of the concepts upon which those cultures were based, we ask you to strive for the attainment of those answers from within your own God-centered self. For it is here, and not in a mentalized dissection of past history, that the deeper understandings you yearn for await you. Think not so much on the necessity to re-create a culture of the past, as one would do if one were given a recipe for the preparation of the perfect culinary creation.

The task before you now is to create that recipe 'from scratch.' To seek as the ingredients the truth as you alone know it ...regardless of the opinions of others ...although they most certainly may be consulted in such matters. And in the conferring with other travelers upon the spiritual path, a certain measure of reassurance is, no doubt, forthcoming. But the creation of the spirit-first civilization is initially a solitary journey. For it is in the dormant depths of your individual consciousness that the true 'genetic code' underlying all creation lies, patiently waiting. It is for each of you who has felt himself driven to follow a spiritual path, perhaps even quite suddenly, to take the time now to explore those 'lost' records.

If you were the Creator, what qualities would YOU have instilled in your precious children? What values would you have wished that they hold most dear? What type of environment would you have provided for their nurturing and growth? And what tools would you put at their disposal so that they might create a world that would reflect, in every aspect, your blessed vision? It is these things which you are most apt to find if you have the courage to dig beneath what you believed to be the 'bottom of your heart.' For therein lies the original blueprint, unblemished by millenniums of misunderstanding and accumulated karmic 'baggage.'

Pure and perfect in its simple truth, the vision of man in his ultimate spiritual expression underlies all that you, through all the untold trials, have come to be. And once liberated from the harness of karmic obligation and the limitation of material-plane orientation, it is this vision of man as pure spiritual essence that you are destined to become. Not overnight, mind you. But sequentially, evolving in your representation of that deeper understanding, until you, and those who journey by your side, embody that vision in its fullest expression.

It is a process that has already begun within most of you who read these words. And this would explain the sense of 'disconnectedness' that so many are experiencing and have consciously identified. Something is changing. YOU are changing. And the full understanding as to why this is happening and the dynamics of how the process is evolving continues to evade you. You feel 'lost.' Out of phase with the rest of the world. Out of touch with reality ...at least with reality as is accepted by consensus, material-based perspective. You have ceased to find meaning in your work; ceased to find meaning in the external expression of "who you are"; ceased to find meaning in close relationships of the past; ceased to find meaning in any readily identifiable future.

Your mind is spinning like a compass devoid of magnetic north. For the direction is not to be found in any of those external sources of 'direction.' It lies not in the ideas, the opinions, the values, or the perceived reality of others. For these are not rooted in "Source" for you. And you COULD choose to run yourself ragged, from guru to guru, from workshop to workshop, from 'healer' to 'healer,' from volume to volume, from church to church ...from now on. But it is doubtful that you would emerge with any real sense of soul-centered knowingness from a stroll upon those avenues. You could literally wander forever and search forever ...if the focus is upon seeking understanding from external sources ...and never find your way back 'home.' A 'compass' is useless to you now, for the 'magnetic north' you follow is in the center. The only way to find it is to cease seeking verification of your direction from everywhere else and know that it cannot be found ANYWHERE else than within your own God-centered self.

Relinquish the myriad crutches with which you have been limping down the spiritual path. Know that what you are experiencing ...your magnetization to a life direction that is seemingly devoid of direction ...is that which your soul-self has chosen for you in this lifetime. And it is that which you will, very likely, be permitted by the Creator to realize in this lifetime ...if your give YOURSELF permission to let go of all that binds you to a limited vision. And acknowledge, unconditionally, that you have set out upon this journey because you are compelled to find the truth, and to manifest it in the physical in this lifetime.

It is only through an unbiased approach to the process in which you are engaged that the results you so dearly hope to manifest for yourself, and for the planet, are possible. Your willingness to trust in the veracity of the sensings from within; your willingness to abandon all that restricts you to the myopic vision of an obsolete sense of self; your willingness to embrace with passion and with an open heart the possibilities that beckon to you, regardless of the fact that you are not yet able to envision the fullness of their expression ...all these are issues which must be confronted. And constitute the 'keys' which will enable you to unlock the mystery into which you feel you have been drawn.

In truth, your role in the process is anything but a passive one. It is you and you alone who have masterminded your participation in the coming times. And it is you and you alone who will set the limits as to how far you will be able to go in your journey. It is imperative that you look at these issues now. And make a conscious effort to deal with the areas of limitation that are restricting your growth and your advancement as an active participant in the Great Divine Mission that lies before us. There is no possibility, as we have said on many occasions, to 'hedge one's bets' in the process of 'becoming.' One can either commit oneself in totality to becoming all that one can possibly be under the coming conditions, or resign oneself to the certainty of a shortsighted future bound by and to the constraints of man's vision of present-day reality.

It is not an easy decision. And it is to be expected that much backsliding will take place along the way, as one slips on the muddy patches upon the path to clear, enlightened vision. It is during these times of setback that one is most likely to lose hope, and lose sight of the momentum with which one upon the path now travels. It is necessary to pick yourself up out of the mud when those instances occur, with unobscured determination to continue to trust the 'compass' within that leads you onward, ever deeper into the center of your own being. For within that God-centered core is the vision that will provide the road map for the coming times ...for each of you individually.

Trust that the way will be clear when you have reached and become at peace with the knowingness within that place. For it is The Source. And holds the answers to questions you do not yet know to ask. Answers that will be common knowledge in the times to come. And will form the foundation for the 'consensus reality' of the Great Spiritual Civilization to come. The encoding is there, within each of you. Yours to discover ...or leave buried ...forevermore.

The choice is not an easy one. For once one begins to unearth the truth within, it is most difficult to return, wholeheartedly, to the shallow 'surface' existence most have embraced, up to now. On a deeper level, you know this to be true. And you, no doubt, ask yourself in this moment, "IS THERE ANY CHOICE???" Is there?

24

THE mission that unfolds before us now is one in which all who choose to follow the Light path are free to participate. The level of participation will be determined by various complex criteria, having as much to do with present choices as past actions. One is not bound, irreversibly, by events and actions that may have preceded this lifetime, although this karmic record does, in fact, come strongly into consideration. In this moment, we are dealing more in terms of potentialities than in absolutes. For much will be determined in the coming months and years that will weigh in the ultimate decision as to what level of participation will be permitted each individual Light worker who has volunteered to serve in these times.

Think not that solely those who have devoted their lives, up until this moment, in recognized spiritual service will necessarily be the ones tapped for the most crucial leadership responsibilities. For there are, indeed, those who have come recently into full awareness and into the fuller potentials as channels of energy and information, who would be more apt choices, should they continue to grow and expand at present levels of acceleration.

Those who read these words may be dismayed at the prospect that some of those who they themselves have judged as unworthy of heavy responsibilities are the very ones whom the Creator would have deemed most capable of leading in the times to come. Awakening in the Light is an individual matter, and happens within each individual as is his time. Some, until recently, were consumed with the completion of karmic issues that occupied the fullness of their energies and efforts. For these souls, it was not possible to permit full awakening to transpire until the resolution of earth-bound situations and the constraints of karmic involvement were released. Once these steps had been taken, however, it was possible to allow certain individuals to be opened and enlightened, and this process has, in some, transpired quite rapidly. For them, the experience of these times is one, oftentimes, of transforming before their own eyes ...to the amazement of close associates.

Do not discount the magnitude of the transformation you may observe in some who now look to you for guidance. For it is entirely possible that among those who you, now in leadership roles, would have dismissed as spiritually compromised, there is an individual who is destined to rise to the heights of spiritual elevation and serve the Creator in a capacity that exceeds, in power and depth of understanding, that which you yourself may be able to achieve in this lifetime. It is for you now to come to terms with your own ego involvements where this Divine mission is concerned. And suspend without reservation all previous judgments of individuals, at all levels, with whom you now interact in this holy work. For, freed of the karmic bondage that has constrained so many, they are now free to step, once again, into the footsteps they themselves cast upon the sands of time, and continue to rise in roles they played in times so ancient they predate recorded history by tens of millenniums.

Parallels have been drawn by many spokesmen and seers, who are guiding the awakened souls of today, to the period in the planet's history that was marked by the culture of Atlantis. And in that those end times came as a culmination of gross misuse of power, the comparison can accurately be drawn. It is no accident that individuals who were instrumental in the drama of the downfall of that civilization have chosen to incarnate into this lifetime, so that full karmic resolution would be possible in these times. The cast of characters has been carefully chosen. For it is in these ancient souls that the greatest potential lies for carrying forth the human race into the fullness of a new spiritual civilization that will surpass any known on planet Earth.

In this moment, choices are being made at the deepest levels, not accessible to conscious awareness, that will help determine which aspect of the coming drama will be experienced by whom. There are many who are younger souls, who have elevated themselves significantly in the time frames in which they have been physically incarnate. These Light workers will be permitted to play valuable supporting roles, and will be a source of strength to the masses who will be permitted to experience the quantum leap in karmic growth being offered in the times to come.

The roles that carry the greatest potential and the greatest risk have been reserved for souls whose Atlantean connections have pre-empted the general selection process. For these individuals, day-to-day choices are now resulting in monumental leaps in consciousness and in spiritual connectedness. And as each comes into the fullness of his potential as a leader in the present drama, the memories of the parallel Atlantean experience begin to crystallize in the conscious and subconscious awareness. Dreams are experienced that are startling and extraordinary. Recognition of connectedness with others often accompanies an unexplainable knowingness that the connection has an Atlantean foundation. It is not uncommon for such individuals to have clear, instantaneous recall of the end times scenario in which they played a part. And to be able to identify those in their circle of contacts today who played supporting roles in that drama. They will sense strongly which individuals within that circle will accompany them upon this journey.

It is for you, to whom they will turn for guidance, to honor these profound perceptions. Do not negate or dismiss what may seem to you to be preposterous, in light of the rocky path some of these gifted individuals may have chosen to create on their road to spiritual ascension. For it is in the profound difficulties, the pitfalls, and the setbacks that the greatest tests of faith and opportunity for transcendence lie. You will encounter many tales of wonder, shared by these awe-struck children of Light. And as they look to you for illumination on their journey, your own wisdom in being able to open your heart and not be blinded by determinations of mind will spell for you the levels you will personally be permitted to attain on your own spiritual journey. For the responsibility for guiding the most gifted to the ultimate expression of their own karmic potential is in itself a weighty prospect. And it is in the choices you make now in providing that guidance that the determination of who will be permitted to rise to serve in their elite inner circles of loving trust ...lies.

It is advisable that you consider very carefully the information coming from these sources now, so that you may determine, from your own innermost knowingness, which individuals YOU would consider to be the harbingers of truth ...and which are the false prophets caught up in the momentum of the times. There is much misinformation being bandied about these days, and credence is something that can only be determined within the innermost sanctums of the soul. It is upon the challenge of that tuning-in, that we wish you to focus now. For wisdom is determined by your own ability to recognize truth when encountered, unencumbered by considerations of the stumblings of the source upon the trail to spiritual enlightenment where one's true identity may be reclaimed.

Weigh with the heart, with openness and with love, and recognize the brilliant Lights beginning to blaze amongst your flock. Nurture these ones with wisdom and gentleness. Seek not to sanction, but rather to EMPOWER. In so doing, you empower others to rise to the fullness of their potential ...and empower yourself to rise to the fullness of your own. For strength comes from strength. Heed the cry of your heart. For it is in the conflict you will encounter between accepted dogma and unorthodox knowingness that your own ultimate test lies. You see, real advancement does not come from following a safe, clear-cut path, well signposted, and free of risk. But in daring to scale the cliffs of one's soul ...against all odds. We invite you to take up that challenge now.

25

M ANY would interpret 'negative' manifestations of emotion and difficulties in relationships as evidence that they have regressed in their spiritual development, and have somehow managed to magnetize events that are not indicative of progress in a positive direction. This would, in all likelihood, be a mis-perception. Such occurrences are more an indication of the necessity to purge oneself of the limitations posed by the karmic foundations carried in one's genetic programming. It is for this reason that so many are experiencing, in this time of amplified energy vibration, situations that constitute opportunities for the releasing of those limitations.

With every expression of negatively-charged circumstance, one is permitted to peel back a layer of accumulated negative karma. In so doing, one ceases to be held back by the influence of that measure of negative vibration. As the layers of limitation are exposed to the Light, through Divine Service, one is able, sequentially, to perceive a growing measure of improvement in all areas of one's life. Before that point in the process is achieved however, there is much weeding-out to do. And the process is far from painless.

Often, one perceives oneself to be 'stuck' in a period that is devoid of momentum, characterized by endless repetitions of the same theme. It would be as though a phonograph record were stuck in a particular groove, and the same theme continues to play over and over again. It is evident in conversations with friends and acquaintances, with family, and within the inner recesses of your own thought processes. Indeed, this is an apt description of what is transpiring.

Life will continue to 'play' that passage for you, until you are forced to truly look at it and identify the dynamics within it. As you begin to see beneath the surface of these situations, you gradually come to perceive the causative emotion, or fear, or erroneous belief that is encoded within it. Once identified, one is able to analyze the part that particular characteristic plays as a major theme in one's life and to realize the detrimental effects to one's growth inherent in permitting its domination over your conscious choices.

You begin to observe that the same sort of thing seems to be happening again and again, in EVERY aspect of your life. And until the transformation process begins in earnest, one is inclined to passively accept that situation as one's 'lot in life.' And so it would continue to be if you were not motivated toward effecting radical change and eliminating the limitations that would bind you to a 'vicious cycle' of harsh lessons. As you begin to identify the common thread within these repetitive situations, you are able to ask yourself "why."

Why, indeed? Why would there be a need to cling to a belief or characteristic that, one has become painfully aware, is not fostering positive growth? Why would the need to retain the 'safe' sense of the familiar, inherent in these repetitive experiences, override one's desire to move forward? Why are you 'choosing'...at a level you possibly do not understand, and feel unable to 'control'...to permit yourself to remain in a position of being at the mercy of circumstances, when your conscious objective is to harness your own inner power and assume control of your life? WHY, INDEED?

Once conscious awareness of the dynamics of these circumstances comes into play, it is possible to release the various aspects of one's 'nature' that has served to magnetize them. And with the relinquishing of the need to 'hit one's own head with a hammer,' comes the realization that a page has turned. Suddenly, these situations cease surfacing in one's experience. And as that layer is peeled back, others are exposed. And the process begins once again, as one is forced by unrelenting circumstances to see the causative reality underlying them, and to consciously relinquish one's need to have that situation continue to dominate one's life experience.

As one's true essence begins to emerge from the prison of self-perceived limitations and false beliefs, life appears to flow more easily. And one finds oneself riding the current, effortlessly, rather than 'rowing against the current' with all one's might ...just to stay even. The objective in these times is not merely to stay even, but to progress rapidly in the direction that one is going. If that direction is toward the Light; if that direction is toward serving, to the very fullness of one's innate capacity in the times ahead; if that direction is, ultimately, to experience oneself in ONENESS with all Creation and to be able to exist in harmonious alignment with Divine energy; if that direction is to be able to perceive oneself as having attained that state-of-being and to know, unquestioningly, that it is consistent with Divine Will that it be thus; then one must be willing to confront the limitations that serve to anchor you into a perpetual state of non-momentum, and to eliminate them from your repertoire, once and for all.

It is not an easy task. And, for most who accomplish it, it will take a full lifetime to achieve a state of total freedom from karmically conditioned actions and reactions, and to function in a perpetual state of true self-determination. Do not become discouraged if you do not experience radical transformation, overnight, simply because you are suddenly willing to look at your life objectively and honestly, and have managed to pinpoint a few common themes amongst the dominant experiences that surface most frequently. It takes time and much conscious effort to achieve the end result. And it is necessary to undergo a certain measure of karmic release of the negative charge carried by these tendencies, to initiate the process.

Think not that you are 'lost' in these times, simply because life has become extraordinarily difficult of late. Train yourself to detach from the circumstances of these experiences when they threaten to 'drag you under,' and look at them from the broader perspective. Chances are, from that more objective viewpoint, you will be able to attain a glimpse of the truth, to identify the common threads, and begin to unravel the 'net' in which you are enmeshed. And perhaps ...just perhaps ...you will be able to know how it feels to float, untethered to thousands of years of earth-plane limitations. And to know the meaning of freedom ...if only for a moment.

26

THE combination of skills and disciplines with which you have equipped yourself in this lifetime have provided for you a unique package of capability with which to enter the Age of Spirit. You may, in the present period, not yet be able to see the correlation amongst certain dramatically diverse skills. Yet, each of the experiences that led you to the pursuit of a particular direction was provided so that you could emerge, in this time frame, with a solid grounding and some measure of expertise in that area.

It may not yet be apparent what application certain abilities may have in future terms. And one may be inclined to assess one's repertoire of skills as an unrelated body of random experience. But you will be amazed, as the drama begins to unfold, to note the perfection in the preparation with which you equipped yourself for these times. Short-lived projects in which a specialty was cultivated could well have provided the very skill that will form the foundation of a major focus of your efforts. Hobbies or pursuits that provided only diversion and enjoyment may well form the basis for the provision of sustenance.

Do not discount any of the seemingly obscure experiences you have had up to this point, nor the lessons that may be derived from them, as yet unbeknownst to you. At a higher level, you know that you have volunteered to serve in the coming times. And your mission thus far in this lifetime was to acquire the capabilities necessary for being of the greatest possible service. Your limited vision in the present period should not deter you from trusting in the momentum of the direction in which life is leading you. That very momentum is an indication that you ARE on track, even though logic may not indicate that to be the case.

In the present period, those destined to participate at the highest levels of Light work are experiencing a disconnection from their previous life scripts. In some cases, resistance to one's predetermined life direction was so strong as to necessitate that radical measures be taken. Such measures would insure that particular individuals, rooted so deeply in material-plane orientation, would be freed of those constraints and able to take up the task for which they have prepared at a higher level. These ones have found that virtually all avenues for continuation in the directions in which they believed themselves to be headed have been closed to them. And it would appear to the outside observer that entire aspects of the previous existence of these ones have been virtually amputated. Know that for these ones, the mission is great. And that it was necessary to insure that these ones, who bring significant talent and promise to the mission, would not be lost in a blindness to and a deep-seated fear of the responsibility they recognize at a soul level.

It would appear that certain individuals have an almost unthinkable level of adversity in their life scripts in the present period. This would be as a reflection of the level of resistance they hold to the changes that must be made if these ones are to be able to function at the levels intended. When acceptance of the radical changes that must be made is achieved, the energy becomes easy. Things flow smoothly. Pieces fall into place almost without effort. So it should be if one is on the correct path. So it should be if one is following the innerdirectedness that comes from connection with one's own highest purpose, and disassociation with considerations of one's logical mind. Considered thought must be given to the degree of resistance one is experiencing within one's life, to the efforts that are being expended. If you are encountering a dead end at every turn, it should be as a blatant sign that you are off track, and should think seriously about ceasing efforts in such areas.

Clues may come 'out of left field.' And these should not be discounted merely because they were not anticipated. Accept the small signposts you encounter along the way as the significant clues that they are. And be prepared to follow your instinct to veer onto a small, untrodden path. For upon it you may be permitted to see the precious vision obscured to those who march noisily down the thoroughfares which are boldly signposted "Spiritual Path." The path of spirit is one found in the quiet, inner recesses of one' own heart. It is not necessarily accessible in the boisterous environments of 'psychic' festivals where the vibration is highly charged with suspicion and mistrust.

Know that inner peace and oneness with the Creator is not a state of being attainable by following a recipe, en masse, with hoards of other confused seekers. One is not empowered by being encouraged to hand over one's power to a charismatic 'leader.' The growing addiction of those who count themselves amongst the Light workers of the coming times, to participation in highly personal processes of exploration in large group settings, has served to undermine the potential benefit in such exercises. Small groups, where a mutual bond of loving trust has been established among the participants, can provide a forum for spiritual exploration that can be of benefit.

The states of consciousness one seeks to attain cannot be accessed readily in a crowd of strangers. The collective vibration of all present would serve to counterbalance the levels that some would be able to attain, and would distort the information that would be forthcoming to these ones. Trust in your own ability to commune spiritually with your highest expression of self. And do not be persuaded into believing that attendance at 'spiritual events' is a prerequisite for your own growth.

Significant strides are made only when one is ready to make them. The timetable for your own growth may not match that of others with whom you share a common spiritual bond. Do not be inclined to measure yourself comparatively to the growth others may be experiencing. For some, quantum leaps in consciousness are permitted, wherein "enlightenment" is almost instantaneous. In these cases, sufficient groundwork has taken place that would have brought that individual to the point of being receptive to that level of spiritual understanding. For others, the process is slower and the realizations balanced and spread evenly over the transformational period of development.

Do not be inclined to feel that you are not 'keeping pace' with the crowd because you have not had certain experiences of which others speak. These are personal matters. And many are inclined to share innermost experiences and visions with others for the wrong reasons. If the sharing of an insight is for the purpose of helping another to reach a particular understanding, thus functioning in that moment as a teacher of that concept, then the sharing of personal realizations would be beneficial to all concerned. However, the tendency of most to proclaim to others the contents of their meditations, their dreams, and the teachings of guides with whom they may have connected ...for the purpose of declaring their purported stature upon the spiritual path ...would serve no benefit.

Such a tendency, which is far too common amongst many of you who are in the throes of transformation, is a manifestation of ego, and must be recognized as such. You do not need to impress anyone with the intensity of your personal experience.

You do not require anyone's endorsement of the levels you are attaining, in order for those levels to be valid. You require only your own inner sanction. And your own confirmation of where, upon the path, you believe yourself to be. The power of SILENCE is an important lesson to be well learned by all who consider themselves to be on the Spiritual Path. For with every word you speak, you dispel a measure of the energy with which the experience was charged. The tendency of Light Workers to dissipate the energy with which their achievements were empowered is a major factor in the lack of progress so many are experiencing in the present time frame, despite great effort.

Many are trying too hard to speed up the process. And in trying to force the energy, it is not able to be expressed. It is preferable to allow an experience to happen. To let the energy flow easily. To invite the understanding. Surely NOT to grit your teeth in forced concentration. Not in demanding enlightenment of the Creator. Not in placing disproportionate, obsessive focus on the attainment of higher understanding. But to relax. Quietly. And listen. For in that profound place of silence, real answers may be found. Not for the purpose of waving them as banners of achievement before one's friends. But for the purpose of honoring the silence in which a particular understanding was found. And preserving the sanctity of that personal gift. For silence IS golden. Perhaps more than you know.

27

"THE calling" is not an occurrence to be regarded casually by those who have received and responded to its invitation. It may be, in a sense, your birthright. But that in no way guarantees that you will manifest the fullest possible expression of that potential. This is determined by what has come to be known as free will. Your choices, on a moment-to-moment basis, serve to determine the level of involvement you will be permitted to carry in this lifetime and the level of evolvement you will be permitted to attain as a result.

With the burden of responsibility goes, hand in hand, the potential for learning the corresponding life lessons. If openness to alteration of one's attitudes is permitted free expression, the potential is great for quantum leaps in consciousness to be achieved in these times. One cannot hope to attain heightened levels of awareness and simultaneously embody the fear and limitation that continues to bind one to a reality one knows, at a higher level, is obsolete. The issue of material plane sustenance is a common one with which many struggle in the initial stages of this process. One may not be able to grasp WHY, suddenly, previously reliable sources of sustenance seem to de-materialize. It may seem as though one has taken a radical departure from one's own life course ...involuntarily. But it is necessary to understand that this level of ADAPTABILITY is one of the skills that must be developed in each of you with the potential for leadership candidacy in these times.

It is unrealistic to assume that one could be simultaneously in the throes of radical spiritual transformation and yet continue in the same material circumstances that defined one previously. Change expresses itself in every aspect of one's life during this process. And it is to be expected. If one does not readily recognize the need for making alterations in one's life script, the necessity for doing so will become blatantly apparent. Often, ones who have ventured forth on the path tend to negate their own progress, citing difficulties and hardships as evidence of that hypothesis. Generally, nothing could be further from the truth. One's abilities to cope under adverse condition are being tested, tentatively, in this way. One's flexibility in altering one's course, one's skills in operating in the moment, one's ability to remain emotionally in balance during situations whose outcome is a radical divergence from the expected ...all these factors are tested and strengthened again and again.

You can expect to be exposed to a constant shift in situation from this point forth. You can expect to experience days when everything seemingly 'goes right' followed by days when everything seemingly 'goes wrong.' And it may appear to you that there is no rhyme or reason to it. In fact, the circumstances in which you find yourself are a direct reflection of the fluctuation in energies in your immediate environment at large, integrated with your own level of vibration in a given time frame. You cannot expect, realistically, to manifest a positive outcome, if your own vibration is in the negative balance. If you are, in a given moment, consumed by fear of the illusion of the loss of material security, it will be difficult to manifest anything other than further evidence of that illusion. One begins to tell oneself that 'everything is going wrong' and the belief thus created serves to reinforce that conclusion ...and build further justification for such a belief. It is not difficult to create for oneself a downward spiral in one's material circumstances when one is caught in the fear of being out of control in this way. In fact, control ...conscious control ...is the very aspect of one's self-limitation that must be relinquished, if one hopes to transcend this pattern and learn this particular lesson.

One must adopt an attitude of total trust when confronted with evidence that would indicate that one's well-being was in jeopardy. One must learn to 'float' above the circumstances and the illusion of that evidence. To not react with 'panic.' To not manifest a flurry of adrenaline-inspired activity in efforts to force what your conscious mind tells you is the outcome of choice. For chances are, a so-called 'setback' is not at all the 'failure' it may appear to be, but rather an event that heralds a shift in direction and an entirely different set of circumstances that offer the potential for significant growth in the aspects of self "you" are working toward at the highest level.

This rationale for what is REALLY going on may not be apparent immediately, when one is in the throes of a given circumstance. But it is hoped, that in adopting the level of detachment necessary for ALLOWING the opportunities for the greatest growth to present themselves to you, that that perspective will become an automatic 'given.' In time, if you approach your circumstances with the expectation that nothing will remain constant and make your choices relevant to the given moment with the information that may be available to you in that moment ...knowing that it is entirely possible that that course of action may be altered in the next moment if circumstances warrant it ...you will be well on your way to mastering the lesson of ADAPTABILITY. In many cases, it will be possible to keep to a minimum the severity of the trials that will, in all likelihood, be presented to you ...in hopes that this crucial skill becomes so firmly ingrained, it is as your own fiber.

In the times to come, adaptability will be a skill prized by those who recognize that uncertainty will be virtually the only thing of which one can be certain. All that transpires in your physical circumstances in THESE times is as preparation for that inevitability. When viewed from that perspective, the rapids on which you may now appear to ride may not seem quite so rough.

28

WHEN the cumulative effect of unrelenting circumstances forces one to step outside of those events in order to gain the perspective of an overview, one arrives at a vantage point from which insight may be attained. It is necessary, however, that sufficient data be accumulated, in the form of related life experiences, before one can realistically assess their significance as a crossroads and as a potential turning point in one's life direction. That the necessary number of learning exercises may not yet have been attained, is the likely explanation for the confused state in which so many evolving Light workers find themselves today.

Know that you are in the process of living these lessons. And that clarification will be forthcoming once the process is sufficiently explored, and enacted. One does not arrive, instantly, at a state of crystalline understanding, merely by having experienced a traumatic and potentially transformational episode or two. It is necessary for 'critical mass' to be attained before one can move beyond the threshold of the experiential to the realm of integrated understanding. And so, though you may be permitted a fragmentary glimpse of 'truth' from time to time, there is the sense of not having fully grasped the significance of all that is transpiring within your life script in these times. And this is as it should be. Once you have dedicated yourself totally to a spiritually focused life direction and relinquished all resistance, doubts, fears, and hesitations, you will be ready to experience the depth of soul enrichment, in the form of life dramas, that will serve to heighten and summarize all that preceded it.

There is a sense that everything is coming to a head, when that moment is at hand. And if, in this moment, you do not yet feel that impending sense of completion, do not despair. For you are still enmeshed in the process of 'becoming,' and stockpiling the fuel for the fires of transmutation and illumination. Trust in the loving hand of the Creator God to guide you through these times. For though the path may appear littered with brambles and the cast-off debris of unrelenting difficulty, it is nonetheless carrying you forward in a direction that is undeniable. Have faith in the necessity to enact the full process, for no steps may be skipped in your painstaking climb toward a crossroads from which past and future options may be clearly visible. Know that, by virtue of the fact that these very words ring true, you are well on your way. And that the lesson, when life is at its seemingly most grim, is PATIENCE.

Many who have come into awareness of the circumstances upon the planet and who feel the sense of urgency in the air are panicked at the prospect that they may not be keeping pace, in terms of spiritual growth, with the timetable before us. They are dismayed at the sense of endless repetition of similar encounters and conflicts. They are frustrated that the momentum with which they entered the path comes seemingly to a screeching halt. And that they find themselves, blinking in the darkness, wondering how they got so lost. Often there appears to be no rhyme or reason to occurrences that persistently provide a repeat performance of lessons that one presumed were well learned and of conflicts with certain individuals that were believed to be complete. These events are as reinforcement of the lesson and a test of one's resolve, as irrefutable proof that the concepts have been mastered.

If you find yourself once again stumbling over that same old pitfall, the lesson has not yet become sufficiently entrenched to permit you to move on. This would be the time to stop what you are doing and examine the dynamics of what continues to draw you into its energy field. See yourself not as a victim of such circumstances, but as an active participant in the co-creation of a drama that has you repeatedly stumbling into the same ravine. Learn to recognize the signs, as you approach these spots upon your path. Train your awareness to send you ample advance warning of your impending approach of them. And permit yourself the time and space to explore alternate avenues of action that may provide the means, eventually, of getting through these trouble spots without muddying your feet.

The urgency you sense, to get on with the learning of these lessons, is real. And this is the reason that suddenly life is providing such an abundance of opportunities to experience 'instant replays' of what appears to be the 'same old story.' Open your eyes and look at it. Really look at it. And give yourself permission to see the effect of your own actions, your own responses, your own prejudices, your own self-styled limitations, your own resentments, your own ego-centered orientation. Ask yourself if these, or other self-defeating behaviors which are well known to you, are major players in the dramas into which you find yourself repeatedly drawn. Take responsibility for your own self-righteous needs. For the need to be 'right' is, more than any other factor, a barrier to the ability to see what is really happening. Your objective is not to be 'right' about anything, but to be permitted to see the truth. Once you rise to the opportunity to transcend this limitation, above all others, you may, indeed, be well on your way.

29

THERE are many in these times who are inclined to dismiss the information about the seriousness of the times to come. There are many who count themselves among the ranks of the Light forces upon your planet who, out of fear, have dismissed such information as pessimism. These ones wish to believe that 'sending Light' to certain troubled areas, maintaining positive thoughts, and encouraging others to do the same are sufficient to eliminate the purging that is inevitable. They wish to believe they themselves have the power to alter the destiny of the planet Earth by willing it to be so. If only it were that simple.

When viewed from the perspective of heightened understanding, one sees that this particular lifetime is but an infinitesimal flicker in a Light that is eternal. And that cleansing the planet of its physical and karmic filth is not a negative but rather a positive. In the larger perspective, it is not a tragedy, but rather a blessing that mankind has been permitted to elevate itself in this way. And that some among you who read these words will bear witness to the transitions ahead and see the higher vision that inspires these changes.

Know that this is not the first time in the history of your planet that such a purging has taken place. It is, from a more timeless perspective, a regular occurrence that reflects the conditions of the times and the consciousness of the incarnate souls in question. In these times, the challenge is to transform the planet into a place befitting a Spiritual Civilization.

It is for you now who have been allowed an awareness and an understanding of the changes to come, and ample time to prepare for your own spiritual transformation by using this time wisely. It is advisable to adopt an air of detached acceptance toward all circumstances over which you have no direct control, and to project positivity that is not reflective of blind optimism, nor based in denial. Know that it is your destiny, by virtue of the fact that you are an awakened being, incarnate in these times, to play your part in this drama. And know that it is your privilege to do so.

We encourage you who are in a state of denial over the significance of the times ahead to heed these words. And to examine your own rationale for that position. It is far better preparation to relinquish the delusion that life as you know it is still an option that can be sustained by rallying masses to consciously will it to be so. Your physical reality can be affected, to some extent, by exercises in conscious focus of intent. But do not underestimate the power of Divine Will, whose vision is not hampered by limitations of physicality, to create that which serves the long-term highest good.

It is just such radical changes which are necessary to create an environment conducive to supporting life at a higher level, in the coming times. And though the purification process necessary to bring about that result will produce trials for those destined to live through those transitions, know that the outcome projected is very positive indeed. It is to that end that you should focus your intentions and your energies in these times. It is the Divine objective of this transformation process that one must begin to envision. You must cease looking backward at a past you assumed would endure ...and for which your entire physical orientation prepared you to function ...and realize that you have been asked to consider a radically altered course. One not obscured in the clouds of negativity that blind you now. But one in which the sunlight of the Divine vision is ever-present.

You who read these words have been given the option of embracing that challenge ...of rising to the promise of "The Calling." The challenge of putting linear logic aside and considering that there is a higher purpose to these times than the amassment of material possessions and the building of a personal posterity based upon physical evidence. The challenge of defying the 'norm' and exercising your recognition of an inner-knowingness most could not comprehend. It will require much courage on the part of those who will play pioneering roles in the forthcoming drama. It will require relinquishing, unconditionally, the reassuring comfort of what is known ...for the privilege of walking a path that offers no assurances. And for the opportunity to dedicate this lifetime to something truly of significance, in a way that that cannot be measured. Yet.

30

Although you may believe yourself to be ready for the next step in your development, the timing of such matters is determined by many factors, not all of which are under your conscious control. That you are actively engaged in the process of readying yourself for that next step is all that is required of you in the present moment.

Know that each phase in your development must be thoroughly grasped and integrated into the fullness of your being before you are permitted to advance to the next stage of your training. Do not permit yourself the luxury of becoming discouraged by the repetitiveness of this phase, for the lessons surfacing within each of you at this time are the key issues that must be sorted through and resolved. It will take much conscious effort on your part to relinquish the fundamental characteristics that pose a barrier to your 'becoming' ...embodying the epitome of all you might be.

Take time with yourself in the days ahead to assimilate the teachings you have received through this work, and to integrate them into your awareness. Make a conscientious effort to consider those characteristics that constitute the barriers that now hold you back. Analyze the realistic alternatives that life poses for you. And consider, most seriously, the option of total commitment to Divine Service, through taking an active role in your own spiritual development and in your preparations for the times ahead.

We are hopeful that you will be able to withstand the difficulties and surmount the obstacles that will be thrown in your path as testing conditions in the immediate future. We are hopeful that you will not permit temporary setbacks to dissuade you from your determination to be all you can be by coming into full spiritual awareness, and enacting that knowingness without the constraints of fear and doubt. It will not be an easy task for many of you, for there is so very much to be overcome. But the mission in which we are all engaged together is very much dependent upon the willingness of ones such as yourself to take on the challenge of rising to the urgency of these times, and adding your own UNLIMITED abilities to the Forces of the Light, who strive for the salvation of your planet ...and the race you would know as mankind.

These are exciting times, if viewed from a higher perspective. And though there will be times of doubt and confusion, that privileged perspective will empower you to rise above the mundane manifestations of planetary transformation ...and remember why you are here. Do not lose sight of that vision when circumstances are at their most bleak, for it is within the context of that higher knowingness that hope for personal salvation lies.

The inner-knowingness you are in the process of cultivating and strengthening now, will become the foundation upon which the entire future of your involvement will be built. Be sure that foundation is solid and free of cracks. Make certain you have constructed it on firm ground that is free and clear of encumbrances and debris from a reality that will have become obsolete. For, there will be no space, within the world of your tomorrow, for the rubble of today's dismantled constraints.

The time for carting away that which no longer serves you ...is now. The time for beginning to build the fundamental structure that will support you in the role you have chosen to play in the times to come ...is now. The time for recognizing your unlimited, Divine essence ...is now. And the time for 'polishing' that essence, purifying that essence, and preparing that essence to serve God without reservation ...is now. And to know ...without question ...that for you, there truly is no other way.

Rasha

Trans-channel, healer and author of *The Calling*, Rasha has worked as a courier of Divine guidance since 1987.

Best known as the inspiration and impetus behind Earthstar, the metaphysical jewelry company, owner/designer Rasha translated her passion for the mineral kingdom into the dazzling collections of gemstone jewelry featured in New Age stores, nationwide. She has been a practitioner of True Light, a vibrational healing modality of Japanese origin, for over 15 years.

An accomplished professional writer, Rasha's 'previous life' includes an international career as an advertising copywriter, a five year stint as a Nashville songwriter and country music lyricist, and a published children's book.

Rasha is the mother of three grown children and divides her time between the mountains of North Carolina and a hideaway near Miami, where she is actively transcribing her second channeled book, entitled *Oneness*.

Additional copies of *The Calling* may be ordered directly from Earthstar Press at the retail price of $14.95 plus $2 shipping and handling. Please make check or money order payable to " Earthstar Press " and send your requests to:

Earthstar Press
4747 Hollywood Blvd.
Hollywood, FL 33021

For future information on the channeled teachings of Amitabh and Oneness as transcribed by Rasha, add your name to our mailing list by sending a SASE to the above address, marked "Oneness."